Living Bright

MATTHEW WILLIAMSON

Living Bright

CHRONICLE CHROMA

CONTENTS

I'll never forget the first time Matthew's home was featured in *ELLE Decoration*. He'd decoupaged the bathroom with magazine tearsheets, there were neon light fixtures in the hallway, and the colours – all brilliant turquoise, fearless fuchsia in the kitchen and unexpectedly vivid green – popped off the page. I'm sure there was a disco ball, some feathers and a mirrored ceiling in there somewhere too. We'd not run anything quite like it before. No one else was decorating with this kind of bravado – seductive in a way that makes you seriously consider a chartreuse bathroom. It went on the cover and the issue was a bestseller. Later, as the magazine's editor-in-chief, I had the opportunity to feature his homes a few more times over the next decade, and every issue was a winner. Quite simply, his style epitomized joy.

It was rare to see a fashion designer so evidently at ease transposing his visual language to another medium. He'd essentially colour drenched and 'dressed' his home with paint and wallpaper rather than chiffon and silk. And it worked precisely, but only, because Matthew has such a uniquely defined creative vision. What he chooses to apply it to is almost a moot point. To put it another way, he possesses such a singular way of looking at the world that, combined with the talent to turn this perspective into something tangible, it matters not whether it's a frock or a pot that receives his touch.

After all, in the late nineties through the noughties it was impossible not to know the man for his fashion. He was an icon. He dressed all the fun 'it' girls of the moment in instantly recognizable clothes that transported you to the colourfulness of India or the hedonism of Ibiza via jewel hues and a supremely romantic view of the natural world. He owned the boho-chic-on-steroids signature – again, no one else was dressing women this way. Dresses, I might add, that always made the wearer feel like their best selves but prettier.

And yet, when I interviewed him some years later, sitting on the sunny terrace of his suite at the prestigious Belmond La Residencia hotel in Deià, Mallorca, he shared his decision to walk away from fashion. No matter that the late great Prince had graced his catwalk to sing in 2008. No matter the accolade of a major retrospective at London's seminal Design Museum. He told me that he needed and wanted to pursue his new, and perhaps true, passion: interiors. But he was nervous. Despite having already created carpets for The Rug Company, wallpaper for Habitat, homewares for Debenhams and several successful collections for the British design house Osborne & Little, he was concerned that he wouldn't be accepted seriously as an interior designer.

Dear reader, I return you to my earlier point on that singular creative vision, which is what I said to him at the time. Against all the odds, growing up in Manchester, and inspired by his mother's love of dressing up, he eclipsed the city's native greyness to give the world his escapist vision of rainbow-hued beauty. First as ready-to-wear and couture, now as wallpaper, lamps, furniture, bed linens and so much more. In so doing, he's generously opened a door that takes more of us through to his magical, mood-enhancing bright side.

Michelle Ogundehin
Author, television presenter, journalist and former editor-in-chief of *ELLE Decoration*.

FOREWORD

So much has already been written about colour – the science, the theory and how to use it in our homes. The dos and don'ts come from interior experts far and wide (sometimes myself included) in the often-asked questions in magazine features on 'how to use colour!' or 'how to add a bright accent!' Yet, much as we do with art, food, music and fashion, we all have our own unique perspective and preferences regarding colour.

Far from trying to add to the somewhat overwhelming labyrinth of colour options and advice already out there, this book is more about the art of colour and how I see it and use it in my own life. I believe the best-looking rooms and those that feel good to be in are those with carefully considered, striking and beautiful colour. For me, colour is without doubt the single most exciting and powerful component in any home's interior. It's the simplest and best way to make your surroundings immediately joyful and uplifting. I hope this book will inspire your eye and further your confidence when using colour in your own home.

My love affair with colour began early in my formative years, when I lived in Manchester, and it largely came from observing my mother and how she used colour to dress herself and her home. She had a natural flair and affinity for colour and used it unashamedly in what was otherwise a rather grey environment. She knew that using clever and considered colour, whether a printed tablecloth or a patent leather handbag, was an instant mood-booster and would go some way towards enhancing her well-being.

I'll never forget many of the outfit choices she made while I was a young teenager, such as a printed silk blouse she would often wear for parties and gatherings with colours so bold and clashing they appeared to be lifted straight out of an Andy Warhol screen print. She knew how to stand out from the crowd. In the late 1970s, she once wore a swirling-patterned jersey gown at a garden party she hosted at home, much to the delight of the grey-clad guests. That printed dress was so bold and full of energetic life that I often wonder if its kinetic, Pucci-like qualities and my fascination with the reaction it received were the kernel of what led me to design for the iconic fashion house later in my adult life. Her use of colour was infectious. Little did I know back then that these daily observations would ultimately form the basis of so much of my life and career in the years ahead.

After learning much more about colour in my studies at school and on a fashion and textile degree at London's prestigious Central Saint Martins, I embarked on what would be a twenty-year career in fashion, during which colour became central to almost everything I did. It was in my early fashion industry days that I was able to develop the idea in which I still believe so strongly, that colour can really have a positive impact on your life. My namesake company, built with my partner Joseph, thrived largely thanks to its handling of colour. The colour I used throughout my fashion career – rich shades of turquoise, teal and everything in between – was consistently

INTRODUCTION

(opposite) Matthew photographed on a favourite walk in Deià, Mallorca, 2022.

9

(opposite) Matthew and his mother Maureen at home in Manchester on his twenty-first birthday, 1992.

picked up by press and buyers. Time and time again my customers noted that the colourful clothes I created for them were uplifting and life-affirming.

Fashion aside, now that twenty-five years have passed and I am very happily and firmly rooted in a career designing interiors and homeware products, I feel equipped with enough experience to demonstrate what I've learned along the way about surrounding yourself with colour and using it in the home. There were hits but there were also a few misses. As we all know, mistakes can provide valuable lessons too.

Inspired by my young daughter Skye, I've split the book into seven chapters, each with their own colour of the rainbow (with a little creative licence). I love watching her paint or crayon the familiar rainbow arches and seeing colour all over again through her eyes. Right now, her favourite colours are red and pink and, in my opinion, when combined, those two colours are one of the chicest combinations out there. Child's play aside, this type of breakdown of the key, most commonly used colours should help you zone in on those tones that speak to you most. The colours you naturally and instinctively gravitate towards are a great place to start. You can always come back to the others later when you need some more inspiration.

From a practical point of view, I'll also explain how I start an interior design scheme with any new client by asking them to think about a few key questions to help me better understand what it is they really love. These questions are fun, quick and easy to answer, and if you give it a go yourself, I have no doubt that the prospect and process of interior design will become a little less daunting. I've also included in the book some of the most commonly asked questions I'm often faced with, which, interestingly, are almost always about colour and how to use it.

Whether you are tentative with colour – a jam jar stuffed with a handful of flowers plucked from the garden might be as far as you're willing to go – or building a colour-drenched haven of eye-popping tones, it's really up to you how you use colour in your home. Whatever you decide, I hope this book will encourage you to colourfully create your own space and make it an expression of you. After all, home is not just somewhere to eat and sleep.

Embrace the colours that resonate most strongly with you and how you want to live. Focus on those tones and revel in the joy they will spark in yourself and those around you. Colour is a universal, accessible and powerful tool to have in your creative toolkit and, just like my mum, I can't imagine living a happy life without it.

MY COLOUR JOURNEY

I'm convinced that I was born with a natural, in-built curiosity about colour. To be clear and more specific, I naturally gravitate towards colours that, for me at least, create a positive atmosphere and feeling – yellows, pinks, blues and greens, for example. I've always avoided, wherever possible, the perhaps chicer, but without doubt more lifeless, tones of beige, cream, grey and so on, as I feel that there is a connection between positive things happening and being surrounded by a joyfully coloured environment.

From a young age my parents nurtured this clear fascination with colour and encouraged me to express myself creatively. They celebrated anything I made, especially if it involved colour, which in turn brought an element of joy to us all. I now try to do the same for my daughter.

I grew up surrounded by a kaleidoscope of colour. My mother in particular was, and still is, a stylish woman. When I was a child, she used colour and pattern liberally and with flair in all her outfits and in the way in which she furnished and decorated the family home. She used colour as a tool to feel good about herself. It lifted her spirits and gave her more confidence. I observed the positive effects this had on her and others around her from a very early age, be it a sharply tailored jacket in a shade of mustard with a purple silk blouse tucked neatly underneath for work or red patent heels and matching glossy lips for evening impact. Either way, her everyday, artful way with colour became a fascination of mine and later a pivotal and defining aspect of my career and lifestyle.

My grandma Rose, a dressmaker, was also keen on colour. I'd happily spend hours on end at her home at weekends, emptying large metal biscuit tins of random buttons she'd collected and rearranging them according to

their colour or decanting them into glass jam jars to create a rainbow-hued storage system, if you will. Her garden was well tended and colourful too. I'd note the soft pastel shades of her blousy sweet peas growing up bamboo stakes, snip them when allowed and arrange them into vases – colour-coded of course – to make her home feel prettier.

I gave similar consideration to my little box bedroom, which was my space to do as I wished with. It became a patchwork of potted palm plants, posters and postcards carefully arranged over a curious shade of lilac I'd picked out, with a painted silver door and matching woodwork.

Only with hindsight can I see how important and instrumental these formative years and exposure to colour were in setting the scene for my journey and career, initially in fashion design and later in interior design. With colour being such an integral element of what I do, I clearly have in large part my parents to thank.

My progress at school from childhood into teens was a relatively straightforward transition. While I had no real academic ambition, I started to advance willingly and effortlessly from nature trails and crafting into more considered art and design projects. I never took to science or maths, and did what I had to do to pull through, but I'd cheerfully spend hours on end painting, drawing or making things with my hands. Here I found my happy place and got stuck into what I loved doing most – creating and expressing myself through the use of colour.

My teachers noted my passion and added their encouragement to an already obvious path. I never wavered in what I wanted to do and remember being crystal clear from a very young age about my future career. This is something I'm hugely grateful for, as I now know how rare that can be. Out of school hours, football and the usual teenage pastimes left me cold. Instead, I'd set about painting portraits and still lifes in oils and acrylics at the kitchen table. I made collages and drawings, and even experimented with weaving, knitting, photography and pottery. My eclectic creative experiments and projects were perhaps far from accomplished but were full of ambition, and all shared the common thread of uplifting colour.

My O-Level art teacher shone a light on me with extra classes after school, noting to my parents that to her, my creative focus and fearlessness with colour was unique. Her encouragement guided and fuelled my next steps. A pat on the back and recognition for good work is sometimes all you need to spur you on. This art teacher introduced me to the theory of colour and specifically how warm and cool colours, when used side by side, could create the perfect complementary contrast. This is one of many valuable lessons I learned and still use today to create impactful yet harmonious schemes. I passed my O-Level art with flying colours (excuse the pun!) and enrolled to do fine art and textiles for my A-Levels at sixth-form college in my hometown of Manchester.

Aged sixteen, and able to express myself a little more, I continued to focus my attention on what I knew would be my first choice of career: fashion designer. I asked myself, what if I could create colourful outfits

(opposite top) Matthew's mother Maureen wearing items from her colourful wardrobe at home in the 1970s.

(opposite bottom) Matthew as a boy, playing in his grandma Rose's back garden.

(above) St Ann's Square, Manchester, 1976.

(above) Natalie Gibson in her print room at Central Saint Martins.

(right) Matthew in his studio in the 1990s, around the time he launched his first collection.

for women, enjoy the creative process of doing so and maybe make them feel a little bit better, just like my mum's colourful outfits seemed to do for her?

At the end of the course, with a bulging portfolio and on the advice of my lecturer, I leapfrogged over the one-year art foundation course that was the usual rite of passage to navigate a way forward in the creative arts, and instead, in 1990 applied for and was accepted on a four-year BA honours degree in fashion design and textiles at Central Saint Martins college in London.

Initially I found it hard to adjust to Saint Martins. Complete creative freedom, in the centre of London, aged just seventeen. I was surrounded by peers who were older than me, with more life experience and confidence, and it took a while to settle in and find my groove. Guidance came in the form of my tutor, Natalie Gibson, who herself was a visual ray of sunshine, dressed head to toe in clashing colours and busy floral prints. She was like a real-life mood board who expressed herself unashamedly through what she chose to wear. She stood out from the crowd and had her own unique creative point of view. She saw my tentative steps and encouraged me to experiment and do the same. She taught me how to use colour in clever ways, and slowly but surely I found some confidence and my creative feet. She became not exactly a replacement for my mother, but a similar guide and guardian of my creative work, which was exactly what I needed.

While on a year in industry away from my studies I found myself working for a textile factory in New Delhi, India, for a month. India was where everything slotted into place. I was utterly mesmerized by the country, the people, the culture and the craft that I saw there. Nowhere else uses colour quite like India. Being used to the grey skies and the more subdued colours associated with England, I was now in a place that was the polar opposite. Women wearing paprika, fuchsia and ruby red, often in the same outfit, were an everyday sighting. Humble suburban houses were washed in peppermint green and a violet-tinged shade of electric blue. At every turn it was an assault on the senses and I drank it all in and tried from that point onwards to distil all that I saw into my work. I headed back home to rainy England, clear in my mind that my work would always aim to include joy-inducing colour combinations with an otherworldly and exotic quality. So

taken was I with India that over the years I've returned more than forty times. It's my favourite place on the planet and I'm grateful for all the inspiration the country has brought me.

Back in London, in my early twenties and still on my year in industry, the much-admired British designer Zandra Rhodes was my next port of call for employment before returning to finish my degree. With her infamous shocking-pink crop of hair, she was and still is single-minded, charismatic and a creative one of a kind. I learned lots more about colour from Zandra and my three-month placement in her design studio. It was there that I honed my skill for fashion and textile design and understood that to stand out from the crowd I needed to have my own creative point of view. This was invaluable training for the launch of my own brand a few years later in the world of fashion.

Post-degree, I worked in the design studio at the high-street fashion retailer Monsoon. Over a three-year period I travelled to India lots more to work on my collections for them and managed to develop a few ideas for myself. On each trip I learned more about design and focused particularly on beading, embroidery, print and colour. These short but regular trips to India were a baptism of fire for me. I was young, alone and on a different continent, but such was the speedy nature of the trips that I had to act instinctively and make design decisions fast to meet the deadlines.

I remember taking a trip once with my partner, Joseph, during which we stayed an extra weekend in a small hotel on the outskirts of Delhi. Heading out one morning, I happened to see three women from behind, walking in the distance, carrying pots on their heads and draped in chiffon saris. One woman wore pink and red, the other green and yellow and the third a darker green shade with printed orange flowers. I'll never forget that moment, as for me these were colour combinations that were bold, optimistic and uplifting in their own right, but that worked even better collectively. This really struck a chord. In the hazy heat of the midday sun these women looked like neon fireflies and they became the starting reference point and inspiration for my own first fashion collection, 'Electric Angels', in 1997.

This collection of just eleven outfits was intuitively sketched out from memories of the women I saw that morning along with a 'nothing-

(left) Designer Zandra Rhodes with her trademark bright pink hair.

(below) A group of women in India wearing brightly coloured saris.

My Colour Journey

15

(above) Kate Moss (second from right) and Jade Jagger (far right) modelling Matthew's Spring/Summer 1998 'Electric Angels' collection.

(right) Matthew, with Sienna Miller in the pink dress that Anna Wintour admired.

to-lose' attitude. Little did I know that three months later, when my sketches became samples and a small show at London Fashion Week was on the horizon, the samples would attract the attention of models Jade Jagger, Kate Moss and Helena Christensen. Straight after the debut show the world's top fashion press and buyers were also keen to write about, and crucially to buy, these clothes, which they saw as full of optimism.

The collection was mostly made up of bias-cut chiffon and crepe dresses, camisoles and skirts. Cashmere cardigans and beaded dresses completed the looks. The magical and unique colour combinations I'd witnessed in India were clear to see, and a number of journalists noted that the collection demonstrated a distinct point of difference from what was in fashion at the time. Along with Joseph, I set off on the journey of growing our fledgling bedsit start-up business into a thriving global brand, which we managed for over twenty years. Central to its success was keeping in mind – and more importantly, in the collections – all the lessons I'd learned about optimistic and uplifting colour from my mum, my art teacher, my tutor Natalie Gibson, Zandra Rhodes and India. In addition, I had the friendship, support and inspiration of two more wonderful women – Jade Jagger and later Sienna Miller – whose infectious, colourful approach to life and lifestyles enabled me to flourish.

Ten years on, in a meeting with another formidable woman, American *Vogue* editor Anna Wintour, she noted a particular dress I'd made in a recent collection by patchworking pink sari scraps together. Anna remarked, 'This dress is special – you should always do a pink dress in every collection!' I took that advice and ran with it. If you asked me what my favourite colour is today I'd find it hard to answer, but if I had to pick I'd probably say pink, as it's brought me good luck if nothing else.

Around this time I became aware of the phrase 'design DNA'. This for me was a valuable insight for the development of my work and brand. Anna also once said it's important to know who you are

as a designer and to stay in your lane. With that in mind, if I were to distil the main components of the inspirations that make up my particular style, I'd cite my parents and the women I've met over the years, my British sensibility combined with my passion for faraway cultures and craftsmanship, all anchored by bold and beautiful colour. I now call these influences the pillars of my brand, as they are the foundations upon which I build all of my work.

I pivoted from fashion into interior design full time in 2016. Being asked to design rugs for The Rug Company and a collection of wallpapers for Osborne & Little gave me the confidence to make the shift. Seven years on I love my job, which is always evolving. One minute I might be designing mirrors, lighting and bedding for my homeware collection for John Lewis and the next I might be designing a cocktail bar or a hotel suite in Spain. It's this mixed bag of projects I love, as no two jobs are ever the same.

My sense of colour and preferences have certainly evolved over the years, but what does remain the same is my love and appreciation for colour and the effects it can have on people. Spending time working out what colour combinations will be the best for each project, client or product continues to be the most joyful part of my job, as I know what a big difference it can make and how it can really make the heart sing.

(left) Matthew's daughter Skye at home in Mallorca, wrapped in an early sample of his 'Enchanted Garden' fabric.

My Colour Journey

FIND YOUR STYLE

Experience has taught me that it's really useful when designing a space, be it for myself or for a client, to do some creative groundwork before beginning the physical, logistical and financial work of the job in hand. Putting the effort in at an early stage will help you uncover your own unique style, or what I like to call your 'design DNA'.

For some, defining your style is easy and instinctive, while for others it might be nerve-racking and overwhelming. I fall somewhere in the middle of this spectrum. Whether it's a struggle or effortless, I believe a wise first step is to visually lay out markers that point towards your design style in order to understand and, more importantly, to see laid out in front of you exactly what it is that you love. Do this before starting any interior design project. If you sidestep this aspect and dive straight into a project, the whole process may become more complex than it needs to be and the results may appear a little haphazard.

Finding and defining your style can and should be fun, straightforward and quick to do. Once you're clear on what it is, you'll make better decisions more easily. Be it for an overlooked corner of a garden in need of a quick refresh, a spare bedroom that needs transforming into a home office or a whole house renovation, it's an important and helpful step. If like me you like lots of things, this exercise will help to distil the essence of what you love most, as I know all too well how easy it is to get sidetracked if your preferences and design ideals are not clearly mapped out.

When I work with a client, I always begin the project by asking them the same twenty questions. It's a simple set of questions I've drawn up that are deliberately designed to be answered quickly and impulsively. For each answer given, I find an image that reflects the response and then pin all the images to a board to create a visual design identity. This board provides the clients and me with a snapshot of what they love most and functions as a springboard for the project to begin on a sure footing. I return to it for inspiration and guidance time and again.

Creating your personal 'design DNA' board will eliminate all of the noise and the options out there that simply don't speak to you. It will help you act more instinctively when making design decisions, with greater clarity and confidence. The board will steer and focus you to create a space that speaks directly to you and your style. Our styles and tastes do and should evolve but a board like this will be a good reflection of who you are today and what your creative ideas and inspirations are.

On the following pages I've listed the twenty questions and shared my own answers along with my DNA mood board that lives in my sketchbook in my studio. It's a gentle daily reminder to me of everything I love. It's a little bit of inspiration I refer to often before beginning any project of my own and during its progress. Dive in and give it a go and hopefully this will set you on your way with a bit more confidence and clarity for your next design project.

This notebook belongs to:

Matthew
Williamson

1. What's your earliest childhood memory?

Cutting sweet peas in my grandma's back garden

2. What's your favourite colour?

Eau de nil / Plaster pink

3. What's your favourite flower?

Hibiscus

4. What's your favourite scent?

Comme des Garçons incense fragrance

5. Who are your favourite artists?

Henri Matisse / Les Rogers / Gary Hume

6. Who are your favourite designers?

Dries Van Noten / Zandra Rhodes / Ossie Clarke

7. Who or what is your favourite musician or track?

'Back to Life' - Soul II Soul

8. Your favourite film?

Into the Wild

9. Your favourite cocktail?

Apple Martini

10. Your favourite city break?

Barcelona

11. Your dream long-haul destination?

Bali, Kerala / The Maldives

12. Your favourite hotel?

Amanpuri, Thailand

13. Your favourite restaurant and bar?

Cecconi's Barcelona and Soho House LA / Boca Grande, Barcelona

14. Do you have a design hero or style icon?

Ossie Clarke / Halston / Dan Flavin / Luis Barragán

15. Do you have a hobby or collect anything?

Painting / gardening / sourcing at antique markets

16. What's your favourite building?

Sagrada Família, Barcelona / Pink Palace, Jaipur

17. Do you favour modern or classic design?

Both in equal measure

18. Do you have a favourite decade?

1970s

19. What's your most treasured possession?

A gold Gucci watch and paintings from my daughter, Skye

20. What's your motto?

You get out of life what you put in

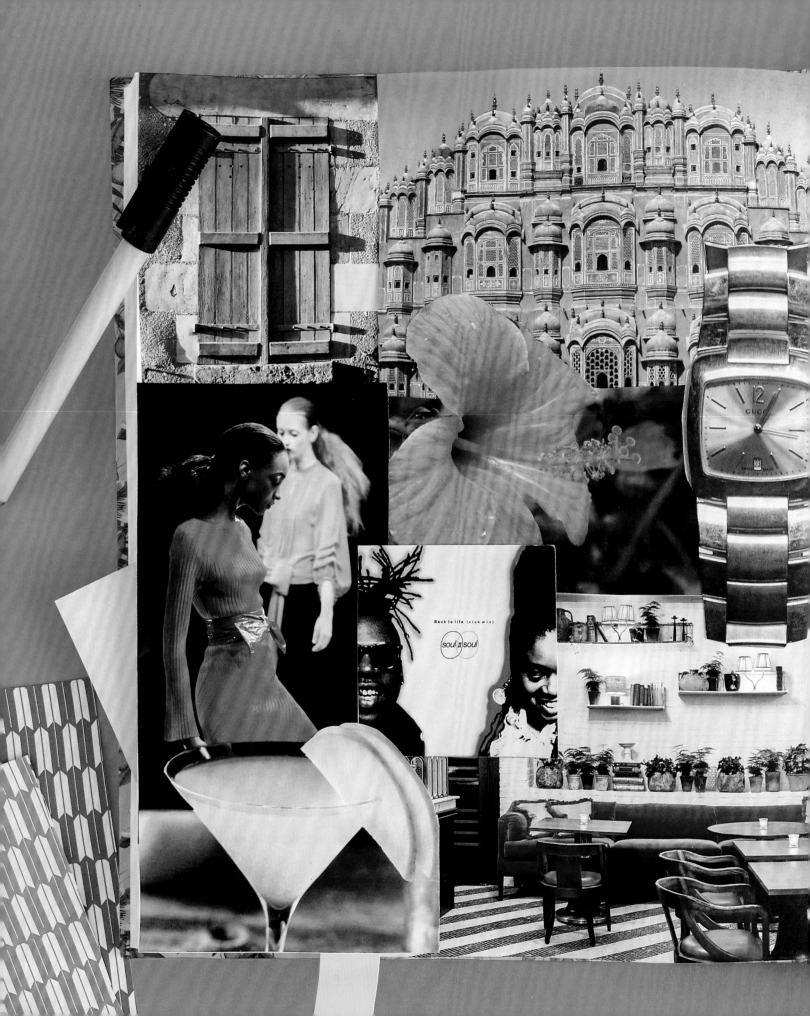

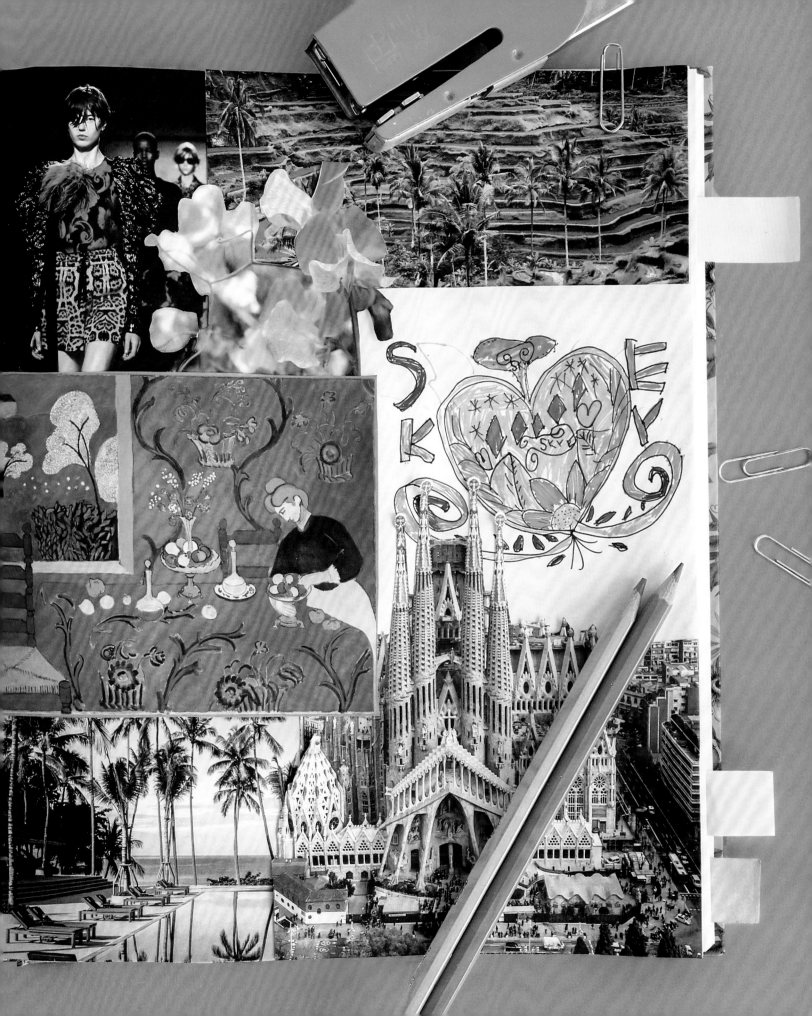

'Decadent, intense and striking – even the smallest well-chosen accessory picked out in red can totally transform a room.'

Just before I embarked on my career in fashion with my first show at London Fashion Week in 1997, I met the model Jade Jagger, daughter of the Rolling Stones' Mick Jagger and his then wife, Bianca. Jade gave me an antique red velvet jacket, which she felt would inspire me. This ruby-red Indian jacket was so old and heavily embroidered with golden threads that it was falling apart at the seams. Regardless of its condition, I instantly fell in love with it, and had it hanging on the wall in my bedroom for years to come. It was mesmerizing and decadent and carried a certain poetic charm. I would spend hours imagining who it was originally made for and what kind of life they must have led. Colour can be so powerful, emotive and even sentimental, and I'm sure this ruby-red gift sparked my love affair with the colour.

Red is a colour with presence. It commands attention. I still vividly remember my mum's glossy red nail varnish, lipsticks and patent leather shoes she'd often wear when I was a child if she really wanted to impress and appear polished and perhaps seductive too. I used red liberally while working in the fashion industry, but when it comes to interiors it's worth noting a few things I've learned along the way with my various red room experiments.

(right) The red embroidered jacket given to Matthew by his friend Jade Jagger.

(below) A corner of the bedroom in Matthew's student bedsit in London, decorated with hand-dyed fabrics.

While travelling back and forth to India, where red is perhaps used more liberally, I caught the bug for decorating with it and set about dressing my first bedsit apartment in London in swathes of red cloth and an abundance of beaded and brocade fabrics picked up from local Indian markets. In what was a pretty basic lounge space, red lace curtains had no practical use whatsoever but immediately lent what I considered at the time to be an air of sophistication to an underdressed sash window. Red tulips in a red glass vase added to the feeling of opulence while a single bed dressed in Indian textiles dyed red contributed to the look. I think I must have wanted to combat the fact that I had little money to spare and overcome the tight restrictions that landlords apply to changing the interiors of a rental. Why should my interior suffer if I can just stretch my imagination and make my rooms a little bit more like that jacket I loved so much, I thought to myself. I was delighted with the result.

A few years later, in the first home that I owned in London, I was still seduced by the colour red. I set about painting what was intended to be a dining room in a glossy shade of pillar-box red. I'm sure I was trying to recreate images in my mind of a bygone era of secret cabaret clubs and

cocktail bars. All well and good in the movies, as a daydream or for the occasional fancy dinner party where you aim to impress, but for the reality of day-to-day living it didn't really pan out. Rich and impactful as the room was, it wasn't really conducive to domestic life. A lesson was learned, and soon afterwards I repainted the room in a more palatable shade of sage green, and sure enough breakfasts and dinners regularly resumed in the space.

With my next home a few years later, I inherited bigger rooms, enabling more scope for interior design ideas. I was still hooked on red and its seductive charm, but this time round I painted only the hallway, the smallest and narrowest room in the flat, in various shades of ruby red (page 28). My theory was to intensify the space I'd use least and make it feel more interesting when I was passing through. It would never look big and roomy, even if I painted it white, I told myself, so this was the way to make sure that it made a statement. Red is certainly not the easiest colour to live with but if you're feeling brave and bold it can have a big impact. I loved that hallway with its bright tomato-red walls, clad with trinkets and mementos from my world travels.

The famed *Vogue* editor Diana Vreeland was a big advocate of the colour red in decorating. There's a famous picture of her lounging in a red dress, on a red sofa, with red curtains draped behind. She made many famous pronouncements on the colour, the best of which nails down just how difficult it is to find the right shade: 'All my life I've pursued the perfect red. I can never get painters to mix it for me. It's exactly as if I said, "I want Rococo with a spot of Gothic in it and a bit of Buddhist temple" – they have no idea what I'm talking about. About the best red is to copy the colour of a child's cap in any Renaissance painting.' By all means follow Diana's advice, if it's just such a red that you're after.

The history of how the colour red was produced for just those sorts of paintings, and now for the paint that we use on our walls, is really interesting. Red 'lakes', so called after the extraction process by which they were made, were historically prepared from the shells of insects such as the cochineal, found in South America. Red pigments could also be produced from various timbers, and occurred naturally as mercury sulphide, or cinnabar, which was mostly imported from China. Eventually various industrial oxidation processes were found to produce the shade and replaced naturally occurring forms, and nowadays it should be easier to find red paints that aren't damaging to the environment.

These days I've moved on from red rooms and have evolved into a phase where I now see red as more of an accent colour rather than for full room saturation. It's rich and intense, so you don't need to load it on to make an impact. Rather than using it as a top-to-toe colour I now use it with restraint to highlight and draw attention to an accessory or piece of furniture that I particularly want to stand out. A single piece picked out in red can do

(above) The pillar-box red dining room in the first home in London that Matthew owned.

(left) Diana Vreeland in her New York apartment, 'Garden in Hell' (by Billy Baldwin), in a photograph taken by Horst P. Horst in 1979.

wonders for the space. I always try to bear this in mind when putting together schemes for whole rooms, and rein in the voice in my head telling me to go full-throttle red. Instead, use it in moderation and as a full-bodied contrast to softer shades. All self-assured designers that I admire employ this trick as it implies confidence and can be powerful and energetic.

Today my apartment in London and my home in Spain both have glossy red beds in their bedrooms to give the room a sense of drama in an otherwise serene setting (pages 37 and 162).

(above) The hallway in shades of ruby red and pink in an early iteration of Matthew's Belsize Park home.

(opposite) A corner of Matthew's student bedsit in the mid-1990s with red beaded lace curtains bought on a trip to India.

Inexpensive cane beds brushed with high-gloss paint in a strong shade make great stand-out statement pieces.

I paint a lot of furniture in my own homes and when working for clients. While I love natural woods, I find more interest in the combination of a natural material with a finish in an unexpected tone and texture. Take the ruby-red chairs and table in my garden in Spain, for example (page 38). These were made by hand in Morocco from beautifully twisting tree branches – charming as they were, but elevated no end by their glossy red finish. They contrast wonderfully with the surrounding subdued and natural tones and never go unnoticed by incoming garden guests. A red vase the shape and colour of an oversized strawberry sits whimsically on my coffee table, and whether empty or full of flowers it commands attention and always raises a smile (page 39).

If you're still in doubt about giving red a go, start with some easy-to-change ideas such as a bunch of red dahlias in a vase, or try a lampshade or candle and see how you feel. It might not be the colour for everyone's walls but a little splash of red goes a long way, and you might just surprise yourself with how easy it can be. From oxblood to cherry, ruby to rust, for me, red in all its impactful variations remains a classic colour and an enduring favourite tone to use in any home.

(above and opposite) The tomato-red hallway in Matthew's home in London's Belsize Park. Struggling to find a suitably bright neon pink for the woodwork, he found that stage paint for theatre sets was the answer. The red jacket given to him by Jade Jagger can be seen hanging in the bedroom.

(opposite) Pickett's House in Deià is one of Matthew's favourite places to browse for antiques. The mix of globally sourced items reminds him of his travels. 'I like that clash, or melting pot of styles,' he explains. 'It shouldn't work but it does.'

(above) Matthew designed the red twig mirror to show the effect of his signature splash of colour on a natural form, shown here against a patinated wall.

(above) A detail of a painted fold-down desk at a friend's house in Mallorca. The colours chime with a portable brass lamp Matthew designed for the lighting brand Pooky.

(opposite) The guest bedroom at Matthew's London home. The painting above the bed is *Tapestry of Goblins* by Georg Wilson, and the bedding and the lamp are from Matthew's collection for John Lewis.

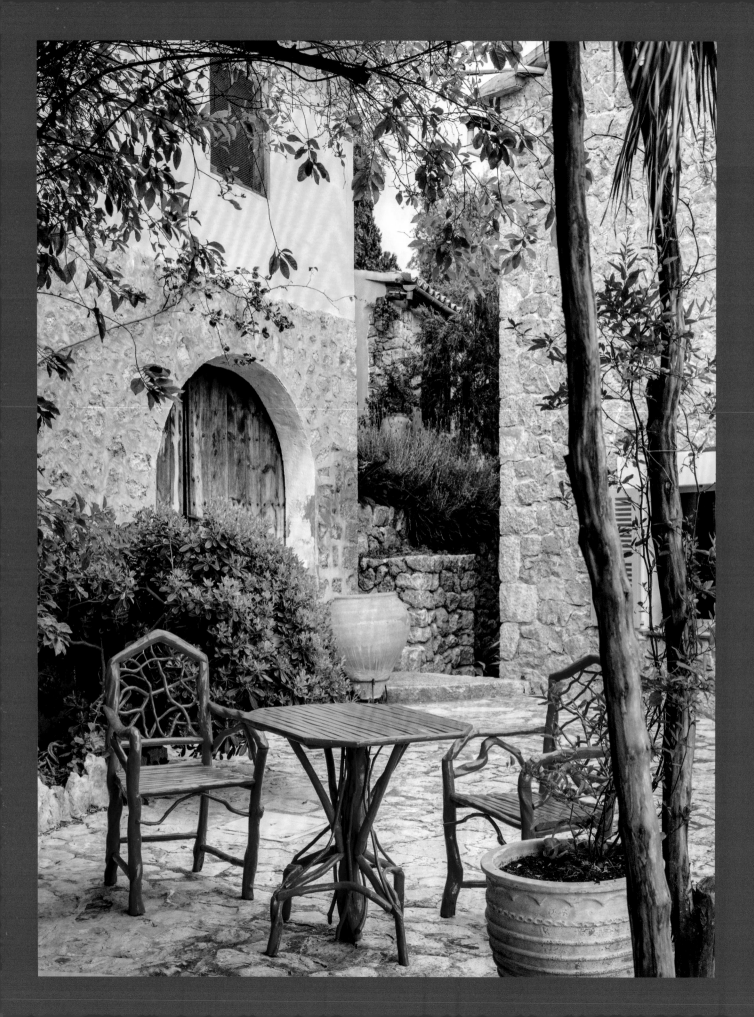

(opposite) The courtyard garden at Matthew's former home in Mallorca. His favourite red twig table and chairs are by Moroccan design studio Now on the Ocean. The wooden door behind leads to an outbuilding that Matthew used as his painting studio.

(above) With a magpie-like ability to spot a brightly coloured knick-knack, Matthew picked up the oversized strawberry vase locally in Spain.

39

(above) Mementos from trips abroad line the hallway in Matthew's Belsize Park flat. The ceramic floral cross and the Frida Kahlo collage are from Mexico, while the Matryoshka dolls were picked up in Moscow. A Fornasetti plate watches over the scene.

(opposite) The 'Leopard Rose' duvet, red twig mirror and gold peacock lamp base are all designed by Matthew for John Lewis.

'Red is a powerful colour to use at home as it commands attention. If you're feeling brave and bold it can have a dramatic impact.'

(opposite) A hand screen-printed framed artwork called
Solar Eclipse by Enkel Art Studio hangs in this lively kitchen.
Matthew is a huge admirer of the studio for its unlikely
colour combinations. 'There is a lot of overlap in what
we look at for inspiration,' he says.

(above) The framed painting of a peacock feather is by Matthew, who is a keen artist. He often starts the design process by getting out his paintbrush and paints.

(opposite) The 'Floral Bloom' duvet pulls together many of Matthew's regular motifs – roses, butterflies, ferns – on a striking pale-blue ground.

Q: What are your hints and tricks for layering up a room with colour?

A: Always try to have a clear palette in mind before you begin a project. If you're a little nervous around creating a colour palette, try limiting your scheme to a few key colours. Try starting with just three colours, for example, and use the palest colour for the walls, ceiling and any woodwork to envelop the space and create a solid backdrop. Use a complementary but slightly bolder colour for the bulkier items in the space such as beds, sofas and large pieces of furniture. I'd reserve an even brighter colour to pick out and highlight smaller decorative items such as paintings, lampshades, cushions and vases.

If finding colours that work well together from scratch feels like a struggle, take pictures on your phone of colour combinations you see and think work well together while out and about. I snap palettes and patterns that catch my eye almost every day. That way, they're stored and ready to use at a later date when inspiration is needed.

Another way is to find something in your home you already own and love; maybe it's the colours combined on a china plate in the kitchen or a printed silk scarf sat in the bottom of a bedroom drawer.

Capturing a palette from a much-loved artwork is also a failsafe way to nail a harmonious palette – take Van Gogh's *Sunflowers* painting, for example, and imagine a kitchen or bedroom painted in a soft buttery yellow with honey, mustard and saffron large statement pieces and smaller details picked out in a sharp leaf green. Stick with the rule of three and expand from there, and you can't go wrong.

(above) A still life with ceramic fruit bowl featuring a painting by Matthew in an antique Spanish frame.

'To lift the spirits, I use yellow wherever I can. Bright, optimistic and energizing – you can't go wrong with yellow in the home as it sparks instant joy.'

In the late 1990s, I made a dress called the parachute gown. It was so called because of the excessive amounts of fabric we fitted from the shoulders to the floor that billowed out behind the wearer as she walked. Although it was also made in cobalt blue and rich saffron, the most popular shade of that dress was a sunny lemon yellow. On a shoot while dressing a model in the gown, she commented how uplifted she instantly felt, not only because of its dramatic silhouette but specifically thanks to its shade, which gave her an instant mood and confidence boost.

Synonymous with sunshine, yellow is perhaps the colour most people associate with feelings of happiness, warmth and positivity. Its transformative and uplifting qualities have always been obvious to me, and recently I've found these properties to be more and more valuable. Perhaps its optimistic energy is more sought after since we've all been through a rather dark and draining period. Shades of yellow are just the tonic to lift the spirits. It's the colour I'd recommend using for an instant boost of indoor vitamin D. From sunshine to citrus, mellow to mustard, there's a shade of yellow to suit most tastes and bring instant joy to any space.

(above) The yellow parachute gown from Matthew's Spring/Summer 2011 collection.

(right) A cover of 'The Yellow Wallpaper', a short story by Charlotte Perkins Gilman, first published in 1892.

It's surprising then that yellow has historically had negative connotations, often seen as the colour of jealousy and illness. 'The Yellow Wallpaper' by Charlotte Perkins Gilman sounds as though it should be a fun guide to choosing the right paper for the walls of your home, but is in fact a short story written at the end of the 19th century that depicts a woman's descent into mental illness and named after the wallpaper of the room she's confined to. She describes its colour as 'repellent', 'revolting', 'a dull yet lurid orange in some places, a sickly sulphur tint in others'. The colour is clearly used as a metaphor in the story – in reality if you paint your walls yellow or hang yellow wallpaper, chances are you won't find it sickly or repellent – but it's interesting that some of the negativity towards yellow still rings true as a cultural stereotype.

Perhaps, like red, yellow is perceived by some to be too bright and bold for a restful and liveable look, yet it needn't be fluorescent, garish or toxic (although I'm never opposed to a glossy flash of neon yellow). Yellow can be subtle, calming and gentle too. Unlike with red, where the range is perhaps more limited, I'd argue that there are infinitely more tones and shades of yellow to play with, from rich honey and mustard to buttery soft shades of lemon. I find yellow in all its variants to be such a vibrant and cheering colour. It's versatile and unexpected and I try to incorporate it wherever I can. Yellow elevates the everyday. It's both inviting and energizing.

Living mostly in the Mediterranean as I do, yellow is a shade that just feels right. You're never far from a lemon tree here, which with its bold and bright fruit provides constant inspiration. In rare moments of calm I can usually be found painting these trees in an abstract style to put up on my walls. The lemon's taste, shape and colour feel directly linked and synonymous with a sense of well-being and go a long way in lifting a space.

While building this chapter and gathering the images it occurred to me that I've used yellow most often in small spaces or rooms where there's little daylight to quite literally bring some sunshine and light into a space. I painted the bathroom in the first home I owned in a rich, golden-yellow shade – walls, ceiling and all. With a brass bowl used as a sink and a lace panel at the window, a bathroom of tiny proportions basked in a golden glow and was a surprising little treat of a room to anyone who used

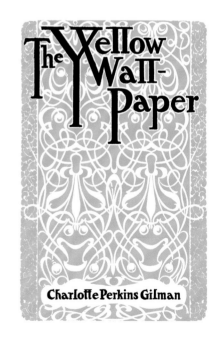

The Yellow Wall-Paper

Charlotte Perkins Gilman

it. I perhaps wouldn't apply this technique to a large-scale space as the effect could be overwhelming, but for this tiny little toilet, a golden-yellow tone was the perfect solution.

Mellow yellow tones that are soft and buttery are the perfect backdrop colour for larger spaces. Think the sort of soft, dairy yellows that you might associate with the top of a bottle of creamy milk. If you are so inclined, play it safe and go for cream for a sense of understated calm, but I'd seriously consider a cream that has a touch of yellow in it. It will still appear calm, it will still complement the rest of the room, but it will set your space a step above the bog-standard cream interior that people so often consider a safe bet, and will instantly feel more unique and uplifting. That's the great thing with colour: whichever is your number one, you'll find there's always a myriad of softer, more liveable shades to choose from. It doesn't always have to be the technicolour tone to bring out the best in a space.

Much like the background layer on an artist's canvas, it's these softer, knocked-back shades that will act as a calming and palatable backdrop. Once you're happy with the background layer, and your confidence in colour builds, you can then introduce more saturated tones to the mid-ground and foreground in your furniture and accessories, again just like in a painting. Clever colour combinations and varying tones really bring a room together. Spending a little time pre-project to sensitively map out your colour depths and combinations is always a worthwhile move. Just refer back to your style DNA and take it from there.

Softness aside, if you feel like adding a bolder burst of sunshine to a room, maybe try a more earthy shade of yellow rather than the more usual stand-out shades of daffodil or canary. In my summer room in Spain, which gets surprisingly little light, I've painted the walls an ochre shade of yellow (pages 52, 61, 62). It's cheery without being garish, has depth but is liveable, and is always a room that we gravitate to as a family.

In the same house, in another tiny bathroom I've used a similar mustard-like shade of yellow on the walls. The tone matches the yellow in the ceramic tiles we used in the space, which adds yet another layer of vibrancy and brings cohesion (pages 64 and 65).

(left) The bathroom in Matthew's first London home, painted a rich golden yellow.

(below) The 'Iris' ikat rug, designed by Matthew for Obeetee, and woven and hand-tufted in India.

(above) The ochre-painted summer room in Matthew's former home in Deià.

(opposite) Lemons in a shell bought from London designer Matilda Goad, with candles Matthew designed for Wax Atelier.

If you're still not convinced and yellow walls are simply not your bag, you can get a burst of sunshine in other, less committed but no less effective ways. I've painted the window frame and a wooden table in my kitchen with an off-the-shelf tin of citrus yellow. Even my everyday kitchen utensils seem to sit happier and sing off the shade. Two previously boring items of furniture now pop with colour and draw in the eye.

Whatever the room, and whatever the shade you plump for, yellow can be easily, quickly and inexpensively introduced to jolt the eye. Vintage canary-yellow metal chairs sit round my garden table and bring vibrancy to the outdoor space (page 68). A sun-shaped metal mirror in my daughter's bedroom has pride of place over a busy printed wallpaper (page 69). Even the doorway to my home office hasn't escaped a lick of yellow paint (page 73). Subconsciously or not, I'm sure my intention was to make the space feel inviting and somewhere I want to spend time as soon as I step over the threshold. In our kitchen, cocktails and cooking aside, there's always a massive bowl of lemons on display.

While I don't adhere to many colour rules when decorating, perhaps a good general rule of thumb is to use the softer shades of a colour for bigger surface areas (the background layers) and reserve the brighter and bolder variants to highlight smaller items or those pieces in the foreground that could benefit from some attention.

Whichever way you go with yellow, it's the shade I'd recommend most if you want to try something a little unexpected as well as revel in its mood-boosting properties.

Although it might not be everyone's first colour choice in an interior, it's worth giving yellow a second thought. Its uplifting, feel-good properties are tried and tested. In spring and summer it's a shade that sings and shines bright and makes total seasonal sense, but perhaps it's even more vital in winter, when the mood is much darker and the days are shorter. Yellow can really combat the winter blues, invigorating your space and enlivening the atmosphere. What's not to love about a little bit of yellow!

MALLORCA

(above) A small selection of contrasting vases and lamps
can be infinitely rearranged to change the look and feel
of a room, as seen on this inlaid cabinet in Deià.

(opposite) Wayne the taxidermy peacock takes pride
of place in a previous iteration of Matthew's London flat.
'One of the consistent threads throughout my work has
been the peacock feather,' he explains. 'I love the symmetry
of the feather, its delicacy, sheen and graphic quality.'

(left) The outdoor living area of the suite that Matthew designed for La Residencia hotel in Mallorca. The floor tiles are Spanish and add to the cacophony of patterns in the banquette seating and cushions. The vintage bamboo chair is upholstered with Matthew's 'Folklore' print.

60

(above and opposite) The summer room in Matthew's former home in Deià is painted the same shade as the bathroom (pages 64 and 65). He liked the effect that the yellow had on his bathroom and wanted to try it out in a larger space, where it feels deeper and more intense. The cabinet is painted in a contrasting shade of yellow with a cooler lime-green base.

'Sometimes just a simple bunch of daffodils, a bowl filled with lemons or a branch of mimosa is all you need to bring a ray of sunshine into your home.'

(opposite) Lampshades designed by Matthew for lighting brand Pooky play off a painting by British artist Alan Hydes in the summer room in his former Mallorca home.

(opposite and above) Matthew's bathroom in his former home in Deià. The lemon trim tiles were locally sourced and the wall tiles are Italian. He painted the window frame, walls and ceiling himself to match the colour of the lemons.

(above) A still life at Matthew's London home. The yellow
vase and candlestick echo the yellow of the chandelier seen
reflected in the overmantel mirror.

(opposite) The 'Birds of Paradise' wallpaper is from Matthew's
collection for fabric and wallpaper brand Osborne & Little,
as is the 'Ocelot' fabric on the pair of chairs. Matthew had one
of the ostrich lights by A Modern Grand Tour in his bedroom
for a long time.

(opposite) A covered gazebo leads from the summer room at Matthew's former home in Deià. Vintage Conran Shop chairs surround a table covered in an Indian block-printed cloth.

(above) The 'Birds of Paradise' wallpaper featured in the bedroom of Matthew's daughter Skye at their old house. Matthew taped the mint-green masking tape up to guide him when he was painting the clouds directly onto the wall, but liked the effect so much he left it when it was done.

(above) When thinking about possible paint colours for a
room, Matthew uses accessories to play with different shades
before taking the plunge. Some yellow and burnt umber tones
hint at the direction this room in his new home might take.

(opposite) After testing the waters with a citrus-coloured
throw, Matthew decided to paint his new bedroom yellow
soon after this picture was taken.

(opposite) 'Butterfly Wheel' was one of Matthew's earliest interior print collaborations with the brand Duresta. The window picked out in a jewel tone behind the sofa is one of his signature tricks to brighten a room.

(above) The turquoise, blue and yellow doorways mark the entrances to Matthew's daughter's bedroom, his partner Joseph's room and Matthew's studio respectively at their former home on the island.

(above and opposite) The multicoloured kitchen in Matthew's previous home in Deià. Turquoise walls, lamps from Istanbul and shades of lemon yellow amp up the IKEA kitchen. To get the red and green stripes under the counter, Matthew first painted the green, then used masking tape to create stripes at the correct width and rollered on the red.

Q: How can I mix and match colours and patterns but avoid the jumble sale look?

A: To achieve a successful mix and match approach it just takes a little more thought and time and maybe a few trials and errors before it starts to become second nature. We all know that you can go into a shop or browse online and select items that have been specifically designed to match. This approach can give a very orderly and coordinated look, for sure, but it can sometimes look a little flat and two-dimensional.

I naturally gravitate towards a variety of patterns in any scheme I work on as they add character and help to tell a more personal story. With maximalism in mind I wouldn't rule out combining any types of pattern, as it's precisely in this kind of curated mix that you'll create something unique. That said, I tend to follow this broad plan when working with pattern. A floral pattern never seems to fail – blowsy and bold or delicate and ditsy, it always adds an air of whimsy, romance or drama to a space. To contrast with a floral, I'd head towards something more graphic such as a check or a stripe, which invariably looks sharp. As in so many areas of design, things that come in threes always seem to work well, so I'd add in a third print such as an animal spot or maybe a classic ikat. Both of these are timeless additions and will sit well in any scheme.

When it comes to using colour across a mix of patterns a good tip can be to refrain from using too broad a palette. Mix up your prints as freely as you wish, but keep the palette tight throughout to create a harmonious core within a maximalist scheme.

(above) Rather than save things for best, use your collection of glass and tableware to elevate the everyday.

'From rose to plaster, fuchsia to cerise, there's unending scope with all the variations of pink, and it need not be kitsch or overtly sweet.'

PINK

Pink is my favourite colour. There, I've said it. A bold statement maybe, but the greatest confirmation I could have that this is truly the case came when I was planning this book. I went back over the copy and images for this pink chapter time and time again. I'd need more than two hands to count the number of products and rooms I've daubed in one shade of pink or another over the years. As this book suggests, it's helpful to get a feeling for the colours that work best for you, and for me pink is it. It's where I feel happiest. I've always been drawn to its charms, although I can't quite pinpoint where my love affair with pink first began. Was it childhood sweets?

Nowadays we often associate pink with girls and blue with boys, but interestingly, as recently as a hundred years ago this was the other way around, with pink seen as a strong and decisive colour appropriate for boys and blue a more dainty and delicate shade suitable for a girl. Frankly, both can be lovely, so I wouldn't give too much thought to this sort of distinction.

Right now it's pretty clear that pink is having an interior renaissance. It may be in vogue, but we all know colours move in and out of fashion. For me though, a love of pink has endured for longer than a season or two, and

(above) An 18th-century oil portrait of a pink-swathed James Brydges, 3rd Duke of Chandos and Marquess of Carnarvon, by Arthur Devis.

(right) Jade Jagger and Matthew shot in his pink kitchen by Arthur Elgort days before Matthew's debut fashion show in 1997.

it's much more versatile than you might imagine. From rose to plaster, fuchsia to cerise, there's unending scope with pink.

While studying in London and living in my bedsit in my early twenties, the first port of call was to give my lacklustre galley kitchen a lick of candy-floss pink. Sugary and sweet, it was certainly kitsch and whimsical. I remember it as a lively little box of happy student domesticity. Inspired at the time by the imagery of photographer David LaChapelle, I wanted a bold look for this tiny room so I added electric-blue and citrus-yellow paint at the windows to jump off the candy-pink walls. I cut and pasted dozens of little teacups and saucers from wrapping paper to personalize the basic white tiles and dressed the space with all sorts of flea-market finds.

After graduation and just before my first fashion show I was photographed for British *Vogue* in the space alongside my new friend and muse, the model Jade Jagger. The renowned photographer Arthur Elgort chose this trinket-covered space to take the picture, and it also struck a chord with the *Vogue* journalist who had commissioned the article on an up-and-coming designer.

In my biannual fashion shows that followed I made sure there was at least one pink outfit in every collection. It became routine, a creative trademark if you like, and pink became far and away my favourite colour to work with. Later, when I started working in interiors, not much changed when it came to using pink, and I set about designing homeware products in all manner of pinks, whether lampshades or wallpapers, furniture or rugs. Commissions from hotels and homeowners alike also got the 'pretty-in-pink' treatment.

Pink has so many connotations and associations that can be quite polarizing – saccharine, camp, girly and kitsch to name a few. There may be some truth in all of this and there's nothing wrong with that, but pink can also be super-elegant, chic and understated if you stick closely to the softer, more blush tones. Conversely, it can also have such a powerful impact if it's dense and highly saturated. I love to use super-bright, almost neon tones of pink in interiors too – think magenta and cerise for areas crying out for some attention.

A few years ago, I was interested to see that scientists reported the discovery of the oldest organic colour ever recorded – a pink

that survived more than 1.1 billion years inside a rock in West Africa. Six hundred million years older than the previous example of a naturally occurring pigment to be found, the pink colour came from the chlorophyll algae fossilized inside the rock. But it wasn't until the late 17th century that the word 'pink' began to be used to describe the shade of red mixed with white that forms the spectrum of what we now call pinks.

These days I'm drawn mostly to the softer end of the pink spectrum. Think of a pink that is almost like plaster. It's become my neutral – warmer than grey and much more fun than beige.

My lounge in London is a large room with high ceilings and lots of wall space. Recently, it's been painted in a soft blush but there's an understated earthiness to the shade that somehow makes it barely even pink (pages 84–87). The colour makes the room feel delightfully decadent, yet comfy and cosy too. I can guarantee that more traditional neutrals would have been less successful. White might have been crisp and fresh but can also sometimes be stark and unforgiving. Beige can be hard too as it's a lacklustre and more sombre option, while grey feels austere and cold and can bring the mood down.

I designed a suite at La Residencia hotel in Spain with a pink lounge a tone rosier than my own (pages 88–91). Unlike when you're working with a homeowner as a client, you can be a little more carefree and expressive and less prescriptive in a hotel, safe in the knowledge that there will be a never-ending stream of guests passing through. Guests at a hotel are there to relax and unwind and escape their everyday lives and one way to do that is through uplifting and unexpected colour. That's where pink really comes into its own.

(left) Model Natasha Poly on the catwalk at the Spring 2009 Ready-to-Wear show in a pink satin trouser suit by Matthew Williamson.

ink garden

Cord/ piping:

PANTONE
19-3952 TCX
Surf The Web

English meadow, lilac: Pleated

BUBBLE LAMP

PANTONE
15-1919 TCX
Dianthus

PANTONE
15-0548 TCX
Citronelle

Blush pink walls
Terracotta floor
tiles

Yellow ocelote upholstry.
against framed botanical drawings

(left) The living room at Matthew's Belsize Park apartment in London, painted in a calming putty shade, Lido Pink by The Pickleson Paint Co. Many of the artworks in the flat, including the portrait of a man in a turban just seen on the left, were sourced by Heroldian Art.

(above and opposite) Opposite sides of the main living
room at Matthew's London flat showing how he balanced
each area with hints of blue and green, and picked out the
pink of the walls in upholstery and furnishings. 'Whenever
I see a gilt-framed mirror I buy it,' he says. 'I don't need to
know exactly where it will go. There's always somewhere.'

(opposite and above) The sitting room of Suite 67 at La Residencia hotel, Mallorca, which Matthew designed. He wanted the space to feel very pretty and feminine, with stronger shades than you might try at home. Painting the original dark wooden beams and the radiator, doors and windows in a complementary grey to the walls softens the space.

89

(above) A 1970s brass bar cart is the perfect receptacle for
the elegant water jug that you might expect in a hotel room,
but also for a punky pineapple candlestick.

(opposite) Matthew's 'Duchess Garden' (left) and 'Menagerie'
(right) fabrics have been used to upholster the armchairs
in a nook overlooking the swimming pool.

'Soft pink has always been my favourite go-to colour for both interiors and fashion. It's become my neutral – warmer than grey and much more fun than beige.'

(opposite) The kitchen in Matthew's London flat. The lightwell is crucial in an otherwise dark galley kitchen.

(above) Matthew's collection of homeware designs for John Lewis includes this kantha throw and 'Rose Garden' mirror.

(opposite) The decorative ironwork banisters pair well with the rug and cabinet designed by Matthew, both of which are contemporary takes on a traditional ikat design. Rather than a 'matchy-matchy style from the same source and era', he aims for a happy mix.

(above) A detail of the pink bathroom at Matthew's former
home in Mallorca. The Indian miniature was picked up
on one of his many trips to the country.

(opposite) For his bathroom, Matthew painted a swatch
of gouache in the exact shade he wanted and took it to
his local paint shop in Mallorca to be copied. The result
is a glowing pink cocoon with views out over the courtyard
at the back of the house.

(opposite) A black wrought-iron bed with Matthew's rose-printed duvet and kantha throw. Bedding is an affordable and easy way to play with print and experiment with colour.

(above) Matthew's ikat cabinet in his London hallway. He has used his 'go-to trick' of putting hot and cold colours together here, offsetting warm pink walls with a cold mint-green skirting. 'Skirtings, picture rails and door frames can be missed opportunities if you just paint them the same colour as the walls,' he says. 'Punch out otherwise overlooked elements with coloured paint.'

99

(above) The mirror-topped coffee table with neon-pink trim and unusual webbed feet was designed by Matthew for Duresta.

(opposite) The mid-century-inspired tweed sofa for the brand is towered over by an orange feather floor lamp. The many colours in the pink tweed play off the rug, paint colours and accessories in a subtle way.

Q: What's the best way to make a space work for both adults and children?

A: Disclaimer: this is not parenting advice but, rather, observations and personal learnings from the past seven years of being a father myself, while attempting to keep my interior design aspirations alive. Generally speaking I'm a very tidy person who likes things to be in their place. The shirts in my wardrobe all face the same way, on the same hangers and grouped in colours. The labels on the tins in my kitchen cupboard all face forward and cereals are decanted out of their cardboard boxes into chunky glass jars that are much more pleasing to look at. You get the idea.

When my and my partner's baby was born, I struggled to maintain the more obsessive interior design details, routines and rituals I had previously enjoyed. With the incoming hoard of baby paraphernalia, an ever-increasing pile of plastic toys and multiple daily cleaning sessions, I slowly but surely learned that a new balance needed to be struck.

After a couple of frantic years trying to work this all out there are a few things I'm grateful for, such as storage solutions, which must surely be at the top of every parent's list. When my daughter was around two, I realized that most things we acquired for her came into the house and were either needed or played with for a relatively short period of time. Not much stays around for long, so don't build wall-to-wall storage systems, as soon enough their contents will become obsolete. You'll only end up filling them with more unnecessary junk. For all the baby-based essentials, such as bottles, sterilizers, nappies and so on, I made do with our existing storage – kitchen cupboards, bathroom cabinets and space under the bed.

(opposite) Matthew's daughter's tidy bedroom with a galvanized bucket and painted terracotta storage pots.

actually need, and soon into my parenting journey I realized that most of the stuff we accumulated was there because we as adults assumed it was necessary or desired. Some items we rarely used. A bulky snowsuit, a wooden kitchen unit with plastic pots and pans and a scooter are just a few items that never saw the light of day.

Rather than restrictions, it's all about editing and managing. One sentimental cuddly friend and the odd easy-to-store flat-packed board game or two makes more sense than a bulky plastic toy soon to be destined for landfill.

In essence, being able to make our home work for adults and children has been about regular decluttering and recycling of what comes in, and handy and practical storage solutions in each room that don't dominate or take over the space and which look good too.

Design kid-friendly spaces with a long-term view in mind. Rather than creating a sugary-pink nursery or a jungle-themed room, which may be cute for six months or so, think about next year and the one after that. It will not only help your space feel less like a kindergarten, it will also stand the test of time, complementing the other spaces in your home, and saving you money by avoiding constant repainting and updates to the space as your child grows up.

I found or repurposed a couple of containers that I liked for my daughter's stuff and set about organizing them in designated spaces throughout the house where they didn't seem obtrusive and blended in with the interior. A wooden fruit crate for her books sits on top of her bedroom chest of drawers, a galvanized bucket was used for her crayons and paints, and a carved wooden chest for the bulky toys and gifted items still sits in our lounge and doubles as a side table when playtime is done. I favour storage that isn't brightly coloured, plastic and purpose built. Go for storage that's attractive to look at, blends in with your interior and can easily be moved around.

Our daughter's wardrobe is purposefully small so that we don't overload it with clothes. When one garment comes in, one has to leave. The local charity shop became a regular monthly stop-off in the early years!

Work with the space you have and manage what comes in. It's amazing how little kids

Ask Matthew

'Green is such a life-affirming colour. Taking references from nature, I rarely design a room or a product without at least one shade of green in it.'

S age, eau de nil, peppermint, forest, moss, lime, olive, sea foam... As such names clearly suggest, green is the colour we most connect with nature. For this reason alone, green has long been a favourite colour and inspiration for many designers and homeowners alike. It's a colour that makes us feel positive. Perhaps its enduring appeal has even more relevance now as we all tend to agree that spending time outdoors is good for the soul; and so much the better if you can bring the outdoors back in with you.

Having been through some troubled times, I know only too well that the life-affirming effects of feeling close to nature can be subtle and simple or intense and profound. For me green is the colour that symbolizes the essence of life and invites an optimistic energy – and isn't that something we all want to capture and bring home and surround ourselves with? As our homes have become more important to us over the past few years, for obvious reasons, I have seen the use of green within them becoming increasingly popular. It wouldn't be a stretch to say that a bit of nature indoors is seen by some as a wellness necessity. This only looks set to increase in years to come as we continue to work and play at home.

Green earth (which derives from, well, earth) and malachite are both organic sources of green pigment, found in places as various as Hungary, China and Siberia. As well as these naturally occurring pigments, and in common with many other colours, chemical processes were developed to produce greens without the need for pigment to be physically dug from the ground. These synthetic compounds often resulted in more vivid shades, and crucially for their use by painters and in decorating, could be developed to resist fading over time. After all, if you're going to go to the trouble of painting your house green, it's no good if it's a washed-out grey-yellow after a few years.

As was also the case with yellow, arsenic was often used in the manufacture of green pigments. Arsenic has long been used as a poison to kill rats and mice, or worse. When used to colour wallpaper, it would often result in the release of toxic vapours that would cause people to become sick when they breathed them in. By the end of the 19th century, the sale of arsenic-laced wallpapers, which had enjoyed huge popularity, not least because of decorative artist William Morris (whose family owned a Devon arsenic mine), was banned across Europe.

(above) The paved garden in front of Matthew's former home in Mallorca.

(right) Matthew is testing out a sofa, cushions and accessories in shades of green in the living room of his new home on the island.

There are many great options on the market now, as sustainability and healthy homes become increasingly important and influential ideas.

The colour green and its direct links to the natural world also have a distinctive influence on patterns and prints. So often we borrow from nature, be it swaying interlocking palm fronds on decorative fabric or a dense and lush print of a tropical terrain on an upholstered fabric, for example. From cacti to palms, parrots to peacocks, the natural world – and exotic flora and fauna in particular – has forever been at the forefront of my mind when designing prints, products and interiors. Nature's patterns lend themselves so easily to designs because we recognize and feel comfortable with them. After all, we've been looking at versions of them in the environment around us for all of our lives, and they often repeat at different scales, making them perfect for fabric and wallpaper designs. It's hard to design a pattern more

beautiful than those naturally found in the great outdoors.

For me it's a given that green has a calming and mood-enhancing effect but conveniently I also find it to be one of the easiest colours to decorate with. The choices when using green in the home are so varied and seemingly endless, yet just as in nature they all seem to sit in perfect harmony when used together. Just think of a hedgerow butting up against a field of grass with tree branches swaying overhead, and you have the idea. Each is a subtly different shade of green but all play off against each other in a complementary and charming fashion. Familiar and comfortable to the eye, green is pretty foolproof if you are tentative about giving colour a go.

Wherever I live, I use green liberally as I know my sense of well-being will be all the better for it. It's my go-to colour and I know it will always work. Classic yet contemporary, it's tried and tested. I remember at our family home as a child my parents bringing back a pair of ornate decorative table lamps where the ceramic floral bases were glazed in a vivid shade of emerald green. The lamps sat so proudly in our lounge, caught the eye and added a sense of grandeur. I often channel those game-changing lamps now in my work and wish we had kept them, as like many things from the 1970s they'd surely be right back in fashion now.

These kinds of lush and dense shades of green feature prominently in my work. As I write I'm creating a cocktail bar in the UK where jewel tones of green appear on decorative wallpapers and velvet seating. They add depth and intrigue to the space and take centre stage without becoming overwhelming. Not only is the space awash with varying shades of green but a nocturnal jungle-inspired theme seems fitting for the bar, where the mood needs to feel inviting and cosy yet decadent and playful.

While deep, jewel-toned greens for me project luxury, glamour and decadence, the softer, more calming green tones on the spectrum also crop up in my work in equal measure. That's the great thing about green, the options are so broad they can be applied to almost any scheme. Paler shades of green are great for bedrooms as they are calming and relaxing and help us settle. In a hotel bedroom suite I designed in

(left) Matthew recently designed a bar in Birmingham, UK, with green gloss woodwork and upholstered velvet stools in a contrasting shade.

(below) The 'Tiger Grove' mural designed by Matthew for Osborne & Little, with sofa cushions from his collection for John Lewis.

(above) A casual outdoor table laid in an English garden featuring Matthew's 'Pineapple Tile' table linen.

(opposite) A cushion from Timorous Beasties against Matthew's 'Rosanna Trellis' wallpaper in a suite at La Residencia hotel, Mallorca.

Spain, the walls are clad in the prettiest little white floral print on a soft sage-green ground, all set off with a lovely patinated effect. Sat proudly in the middle of the room is a vintage wooden bed painted in a striking shade of blue, neatly throwing aside the myth that blue and green should never be seen together (pages 112 and 113). Soft and subdued, the green is the perfect colour to combine with almost all others while aiding a restful night's sleep. This small example also goes some way to proving the one main thing I'd like you to take away from this book: that there's no need for colour rules or any dos and don'ts. It's much more fun to go with your instincts and play with tones you love and use your own judgment.

Back in England, my garden is a simple, understated affair with a small grass lawn and a tumbling evergreen bush. On a sunny summer's day there's nothing I like more than a dinner outdoors. Cocooned in a backdrop of green foliage I instantly feel calm. Even indoors on a more often than not *not*-sunny day (this is England, after all), just a glance out into the garden, knowing it's there for when the sun does design to shine, gives a daily dose of feel-good factor.

With all that in mind, it's perhaps no surprise that my own bedroom, which was my latest decorating job before this book went to print, is painted top-to-toe green (pages 118–119). A mid-tone of mint, called Tequila Green, it is at once crisp and striking yet evokes a feeling of calm. Where the ceiling drops down low, it is painted with a moodier and more intense Basilica Green. An eclectic mix of rugs, artworks, bed linens and plants all sit in harmony together, unified by the colour green. The soothing properties of a symphony of greens were for me the only choice in a personal space I use every day and where I want to feel calm and well rested. I always feel good in this newly painted green room.

Eda tor - chase
style wallpaper

(above and opposite) The bedroom of the suite that Matthew designed for La Residencia hotel in Mallorca. The bedspread is his 'Lyrebird' design, with 'Rosanna Trellis' wallpaper. Matthew has papered between the painted ceiling beams with a star design in the same colourway as the walls for another layer of pattern, which emulates the night sky.

(*opposite*) Skye's bedroom in their former Mallorca home. The trimmed canopy for the bed was made by a local friend on the island and simply pinned up over a painted brass frame. 'It's a very grand gesture but done in a DIY way, and becomes the focal point for an otherwise nondescript room,' Matthew explains. Perfect for a little girl's bedroom.

(*above*) Feeling that the 'Almudaina' wallpaper from Osborne & Little in the main living area of his former house was a little grey and flat, Matthew set to work painting it with acrylic paint. 'Don't be afraid to pimp designs!' he says.

'For me, green feels like the colour most connected to nature. Wherever I live, I use it liberally, as I know my sense of well-being will be all the better for it.'

(opposite) The exterior of Matthew's former home in Mallorca, seen through an abundance of planting. Matthew was helped by British garden designers the Rich brothers to create the lush space.

(right) The latest iteration of Matthew's bedroom in his London flat is layered in jewel-like shades of green, and deliberately designed to induce restful sleep. The main wall colour is Tequila Green by The Pickleson Paint Co., with the ceiling, shutters and skirting board in a darker gloss. Matthew didn't want it to look too coordinated or matching. The yellow-ochre bed linen jolts the eye and 'throws things off a little'.

(opposite) Matthew's London shop opened on Bruton Street in 2004. A glass box housed an indoor jungle with an 18th-century sofa and Chinoiserie wallpaper from de Gournay.

(above) A marble-topped chest in Matthew's London bedroom holds various trinkets. The mirror, lamp and candle were designed by Matthew and the pot was chosen for its 'William Morris' qualities.

(opposite and above) Two views of a bar that Matthew recently
designed in Birmingham, UK. The bar consists of three different
spaces, each with a distinct atmosphere. Matthew calls this area
the Eden Bar. Various shades and textures of green include the
'Jungle Faunacation' wallpaper by Divine Savages, green velvet
banquettes and stools, and six botanical paintings by Molly
Coath (opposite), all set against a poured black cement floor.

(opposite and above) Two views of the raised 'Cabana' area
in the Birmingham bar. The wallpaper is 'Forbidden Bloom'
in the black colourway by Divine Savages. This area was
designed to be overtly feminine, with a garden trellis ceiling
painted in Basilica Green, the same colour as Matthew's
London bedroom (pages 118–119). A hanging garden of plants is
suspended from the ceiling, dotted with glass domes of light.

(opposite) The 'Enchanted Garden' bedding, circular rose mirror and 'Planet' glass pendant lights, all designed by Matthew, combine for a cool-toned finish in this bedroom.

(above) The 'Deya Meadow' wallpaper is Matthew's best-selling wallpaper design for Osborne & Little. Flowers, butterflies and grasses evoke the area surrounding his Mallorca home in spring.

(above) The 'Tiger Grove' mural was designed by
Matthew for Osborne & Little, with the sofa cushions
and lighting also his designs. The patinated walls
offer a textural contrast to the plush sofa.

(opposite) The 'Riyadh Star' rug and 'Menagerie' cushion
are both designed by Matthew. 'The rug and chair are
all you need for a room of such scale and grandeur,' says
Matthew. 'The walls do a lot of the work in terms of
visual interest, so know when to stop.'

(right) This 2006 photo shows Matthew's previous home in North London, and was on the cover of *ELLE Decoration* magazine. The floor is white rubber and he used the same neon-pink theatre paint around the doors as in the hallway of his current London flat (page 32). The gold mirror has also come with him to his new home. 'It's funny to see how it's all there from the beginning,' he says.

Q: How can I create a similar look and style to yours if I live in a new-build home?

A: This is an interesting question as I'm naturally drawn to homes that have some age and character. That said, my work is always about balance. If something contemporary is featured prominently, I like to balance it with something old. I'd contrast a powerful colour against something soft, and I think detailed patterns work best against something plain. If a texture is shiny or lacquered I'd tend to mix it with something raw and natural.

In a new-build space with few features I'd start with the larger surface areas or items in the room – I'm talking walls, floors and big pieces of furniture. Reclaimed, vintage or family heirlooms can be a great place to start. Imagine a lounge where the walls are white and the ceiling low. I'd think about a large vintage rug with decorative details that feel antique. Think about where you can add contrasts. A rounded and slouchy button-backed sofa in a traditional style would jar nicely with the sharp corners and angles of a new-build space. A patinated or retro console or cabinet would again provide more layers. Vintage and antique furniture need not be fussy or old-fashioned and in fact when smaller decorative details such as framed artworks, vases and so on are strategically added to a new space, it's exactly this kind of contrast that will bring the space to life.

While my home in London has high ceilings and Victorian architectural details that add to its charm, cleverly sourced items will work just as well, if not even better, in a new-build space as the contrast between old and new will be even more apparent.

I've always believed that when you mix up items from different eras and genres it's in that mix that you can create a space that has more soul. Keep an open mind and source what you love from different decades. While it may take a little longer, you'll be sure to create a space with more character that's uniquely yours.

(above) This room in a client's home used to be a plain thoroughfare with little decoration.

'Orange is perhaps the colour that I associate most with the 1970s. Bold and bright, rich and retro, it packs a juicy punch.'

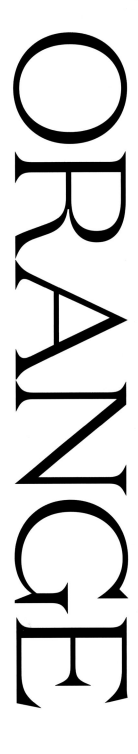

F or me, orange has some lovely connotations – warm evening sunsets and fruit trees in my garden, both of which I'm lucky enough to witness all year round in my new hilltop home in Deià, Mallorca. From pumpkin to peach, it's a rich, ripe, joyful and impactful colour, yet for some reason a little overlooked when it comes to interiors.

Orange is also the colour I most associate with my favourite design decade, the 1970s. I once created a collection inspired by that decade when I was design director at Emilio Pucci and remember its lacklustre reaction from the majority of the press, who seemed to consider the references, and the use of orange in particular, to be a little intense and somewhat retrospective. Like Marmite, you either love it or you don't. But love it or loathe it, orange need not feel harsh, intense or reminiscent of a throwback.

The colour orange in English is named after the fruit, which was introduced to the country from Spain in the 15th century. Before then, what we think of as orange was simply called yellow-red. That's not to say that there were no orange pigments in use. Quite the opposite in fact, as mineral pigment with a distinct orange hue, known as realgar, was

(above) Lady Lilith (1866–68) by the Pre-Raphaelite painter Dante Gabriel Rossetti.

(right) A cocktail dress from the Matthew Williamson Spring/Summer 2012 fashion show in the Turbine Hall of London's Tate Modern.

used by the ancient Egyptians to paint their tombs. Van Gogh was a great proponent of using orange in his paintings as a contrast to his rich blues. Perhaps the artistic movement most associated with orange, however, is the Pre-Raphaelites, whose strong, flame-haired women were often draped in the gleaming shade.

Orange in its purest punch-packing form is bold, fresh and optimistic, plus there are many more variants and softer, nuanced options to go for than the literal straight-up (orange) juicy shade. Think instead of the two other sides of the orange spectrum. Darker, richer shades of ochre, cinnamon and rust, for example, are always super-chic. Just think of those Pre-Raphaelites' hair. Then there are the paler, peachier tones such as apricot and coral, which can help to broaden orange's appeal and still make a statement.

I've never designed a space to date where orange is the predominant colour. I tend to shy away from it instinctively, as I guess it just feels a bit ... much. Instead, I've used it over the years more as an uplifting interior accent, and back in the day for the occasional evening gown as a somewhat unusual alternative to the more popular reds and pinks. Unlike my Pucci collection, which was perhaps too literally inspired by the 1970s, I remember much more fondly the opening sequence of a collection I made a few years later. The collection was set in the imposing concrete interior of the Turbine Hall of the Tate Modern art gallery in London, and orange featured heavily, but in a more subtle and nuanced way, with brick-toned jumpsuits and rust-coloured evening gowns lending a more sophisticated air. These deeper – spicier if you like – orange tones, combined with accents of mustard, blush pink and electric blue, have always stood out in my mind and remained my favourite palette from my fashion days.

Back in my London home, I have two paintings that are both predominantly orange in tone, continuing the same palette from fashion to interiors, as is so often the case in my work. Their titles are orange-orientated too (pages 140 and 141). The orange door and the orange tree paintings sit comfortably propped against an expansive plaster-pink wall. Here the earthy orange tones in the artworks feel totally liveable and chic, while also feeling a little unusual. Although I'm yet to design a space in top-to-toe orange, textiles, artworks and accessories in sister shades of orange can feel rustic and naturalistic, adding warmth, depth and interest to a space.

Back in Spain, my new home is yet to undergo its pending interior transformations (I'm sticking to my own rules and currently busily assembling a mood board based on my style DNA) but there are a couple of early signs that orange will play its part. Keen to avoid the commonplace codes of Balearic living, where white and beige with natural woods and the occasional spot of blue take precedence, I want the space to feel more individual, less typical and, ultimately, more me. Orange will do just the trick. The kitchen I've inherited is largely covered in oxblood-red ceramic tiles, which I'm keen to keep. For the walls and ceiling around them, I've chosen a golden mustard-like tone that feels somewhere between yellow and orange and will provide a vibrant and bold yet liveable complementary colour.

Over in the adjoining lounge and still channelling my 1970s fascination, the walls will be blush pink, providing the perfect backdrop for brick and mustard velvet sofas reminiscent of the palette in that fashion show that I remember fondly. Orange and amber vintage Murano glass lights will enhance the space with their golden glow. When orange is used in a less literal way it can make for a very sophisticated and inviting space to be.

In the lounge now sits a hazy 1970s-inspired photograph of Californian palm trees silhouetted against an orange sunset sky. Perched in front on a wooden chest is a 1970s Spanish glass vase with orange markings (page 146). It's a little bit retro and perhaps even contains a nod to my childhood home. It's a decorative spot that feels personal to me and is masquerading right now as a 3D mood board to muse over and contemplate my orange-hued interior before the renovations begin in earnest.

(above) A 1970s Italian Murano glass pendant light shimmers in the lobby of the bar Matthew recently designed in Birmingham, UK.

Vivid   Julia Green & Armelle Habib

JULIAN SCHNABEL

Frida Kahlo

(opposite) Stacks of interior-decoration magazines on the wall-hung bookcase on one side of Matthew's London living room provide useful inspiration for upcoming projects. The painting is *The Orange Door* by artist Florence Hutchings.

(above) On the opposite side of the room, *Orange Tree* by Jonathan Schofield hangs above a 1970s American cane sideboard painted in mint green.

141

'If orange feels too bright, consider earthy or spicy tones such as brick, terracotta, saffron and cinnamon.'

(opposite) Matthew's 'Oh So Sisco' rug was inspired by a trip to San Francisco, and is a more graphic take on his favourite peacock motif.

(opposite) Before he painted it green, Matthew's London bedroom was papered with his vibrant 'Habanera' wallpaper for an uplifting, tropical effect.

(above) A framed painting of a parrot introduces colour to a display atop a cabinet, alongside a ceramic bubble lamp for John Lewis.

(above) A 1970s vase sits on an antique Spanish chest in Matthew's new lounge in Deià, in front of a print by photographer Kate Bellm. The deep chest is the perfect place to keep Skye's toys that might otherwise clutter up the room.

(opposite) Floor-to-ceiling mirror tiles clad the chimney breast in Matthew's previous North London home. The mirrored chair was 'too good to pass up' at Primrose Hill antiques store Tann-Rokka. Mirrors reflecting lots of external light can make rooms feel more spacious.

(opposite) When Matthew first moved into his Belsize Park flat he chose his metallic parrot-print wallpaper for the lounge, seen here with an African feathered headdress above the fireplace.

(above) Framed trinkets and photos set against a bright orange wall in Matthew's old student bedsit in London.

(above) A lilac and orange print by Matthew's friends at Enkel Art Studio hangs above an elegant white sofa.

(opposite) Matthew's 'Chateau' wallpaper looks particularly imposing on a dark ground. Bright colours often sing out even more clearly when set against shades of black and chocolate brown.

(above) Matthew is currently trying out shades of orange in his new home in Mallorca. Velvet upholstery in a cheering shade can breathe new life into tired pieces of furniture.

(opposite) An iron daybed is a neutral setting for zingy shades of upholstery. Matthew's 'Coralino' wallpaper and fabric is shown here.

Q: If you could only pick three things you'd do on a tight budget to improve or update a room, what would they be?

A: I'm a firm believer that while a full top-to-toe renovation or redesign of a room can bring with it many wonderful things, equally it can sometimes be the smaller changes that make all the difference. In fact, when I work on projects for clients I try to explain to them that sometimes it can be the tiniest of details that can be the real game-changers. I'd suggest that colour or pattern in the walls, lighting and artworks are the easy updates and finishing touches, like jewellery with an outfit, that will take little effort but have maximum impact.

Colour is the tool we can all access for the most dramatic change we can make to any space. While it's easy to stick with what we know and like (I often default when painting rooms to my comfort-zone colours of soft pinks and greens) it's also a good idea from time to time to challenge the familiar and try something new. Wallpaper is a great way to update a room, but can be expensive. Paint needn't be if you colour match a premium brand and swap in something more economical. Pick out a colour from a favourite wallpaper and replicate it in paint instead.

Artworks can bring huge impact to a space and really reflect and reveal an aspect of the owner's personality and taste. For this reason, I sometimes find it quite hard to make a commitment to artworks myself. Rather than seeing art as a lofty subject and a hard nut to crack, I've made a breakthrough recently on an easy and inexpensive approach. Look at books in your own bookcase for

(opposite) The oil painting of a musician in a hat was picked up for a song in a street market in Mallorca.

images you love. Why not photograph or scan those images and frame them yourself? I've done this for a hotel suite using a series of botanical drawings of flora and fauna from a favourite book by a favourite artist. Placed in thin gilt frames they look a million dollars yet cost next to nothing. You could use magazine cuttings, postcards and gift cards for smaller framed artworks, or even wrapping paper. I recently came across some hand-crafted marble wrapping papers, which are waiting for the perfect frames. I can imagine them as a series of three framed papers in a row as the perfect welcoming artwork installation for a long entrance hallway or as a watery piece of artwork for a blank bathroom wall. Finally, if nothing comes to mind, get out your paintbrush. I've done this for my own home by painting over an existing canvas I found at a flea market where the frame was wonderful but the subject matter less so. It's far from a Picasso but it's personal, and the colours work well as I've chosen them to complement the space.

Lighting is always at the top of a designer's to-do list. They know the power of good lighting to set a mood and create atmosphere. While detailed lighting plans at the start of a project are always wise, you can also easily top up on the lighting within a finished space, which needn't break the bank but will elevate the spot no end. Battery-operated lamps are now well designed and quite commonplace. I've dotted three of the portable lamps I designed for Pooky around my London lounge (on a drinks trolley for glamorous glow, a coffee table for a focal point and a dining table for a decadent, dimly lit dinner), which all give the space a wonderfully opulent glow.

'Purple can be rich and evocative or dark and intense, though I tend to favour its paler, more knocked-back relatives such as lavender and lilac.'

PURPLE

I don't like the colour purple much and I make no apologies for that. For me, it's never really appealed. I'm not keen on aubergines, blueberries or red grapes for that matter either. I'm not sure if that's just coincidence or whether there's something more in it. Either way, purple is a colour I'm rarely drawn to.

I've always found purple to be one of the most challenging colours to integrate into an interior scheme. Its dark, intense tone for some reason feels heavy with an almost sombre quality. 'Who would want that in the space where they live?' I often find myself asking. It's important to know what you love but equally useful to know what you don't like too. Purple for me is a hard nut to crack.

When thinking about my resistance to the colour for this chapter, I recalled my school uniform jumper being a distinct shade of purple. I also remember the obligatory Sunday church service as a child, where I was an altar boy, and the priest would be cloaked in the shade too. Both of these are childhood memories that are far from my happiest. It may be that these memories still have resonance now, pushing me away from a shade that others find appealing, or there may simply be no rhyme or reason as to why *(right)* Portrait of Elizabeth I of England wearing purple, painted *c.* 1585–90 by an unknown artist.

(below) The entrance to the Birmingham bar recently designed by Matthew is intended to give off a low-lit cabaret vibe. The wallpaper is 'Gershwing Macaw' by Divine Savages.

we are attracted to certain colours and to others less so. I'm sure Freud would have something to say about all of this.

Snail mucus might not be the most appealing source of colour pigment, but that's exactly what was used in classical antiquity to produce purple paint. The extremely high price of extracting such an unusual resource is what led to purple being associated with the wealthiest in society, from bishops to kings and emperors. I was interested to discover that in other parts of the world, such as Polynesia and Costa Rica, similar dyes were made from sea urchins and sea snails respectively. A purple dye can be made from a variety of lichen that grows around the Mediterranean, called archil, while blackberries, mulberries and other fruits can also be used, although these dyes tend to fade quickly in sunlight. Perhaps I'll give it a go myself!

Although I don't wear purple or design with it much either, I can objectively see its merits. Rich and evocative, it would surely set the mood for a dark and intense interior if that is your intention. While I was finishing the copy for this book, I was also nearing the end of designing a cocktail bar in the UK. I'd designed the main areas of the bar in my favourite go-to eau de nil tones and shades of decadent electric and midnight blue, but for the lobby and entrance I surprised myself by plumping for purple. Well, not exactly purple as such, but more of berry-toned deep red, which is as near to purple as I'm likely to get. I think I must have wanted to shock people with an unexpected use of a colour I'm less known for.

When I thought on it some more and looking back at the space, I realized that not only do I really like the atmosphere it gives, with its rich and moody palette, but also I stand by the idea that it was the right choice for an inviting and intriguing entrance. The richly painted and papered plum walls set the scene for what promises to be a decadent late-night spot where good times will be had. Proof indeed that colours, and more importantly our reaction to them, can change over time and that sometimes stepping out of your usual colour comfort zone can be surprisingly liberating.

My first piece of advice is to use purple sparingly. This is the approach I've taken when designing with the colour. Fabric on a gilt sofa springs to mind, or to bring out the hue of sunbirds painted purple in a wallpaper design for a stately home bedroom I designed in Oxfordshire (pages 170 and 171). I've dipped my toe into purple as a print design for fashion, namely roaming leopards and peacock fronds used on slinky silk-jersey dresses, and more recently as leopard spots on a lampshade print I designed for the lighting brand Pooky.

While still in the realm of purple, I tend to prefer its paler, more knocked-back relatives such as lavender and lilac. My old bedroom in Spain was painted a soft shade of lavender (pages 162–165). I'm a little stumped as to why I went for the shade, given all the other colours of the rainbow I love much more. But choose it I did. Perhaps I wanted to try something new and come out of my comfort zone with a colour I hadn't used before? Perhaps I wanted to see if it might have the allure that pink and green have for me, and whether I'd grow to love it? The colour worked well in the space but it didn't make my heart sing, and I know that colour can and should, so it didn't remain for long. That's one of the great things about using colour, particularly on walls: it can easily be changed at relatively little cost if you feel you've got it wrong, so switch it up as often as you wish.

In the end, I stuck with the lavender shade for a while since it was soothing and restful, but as I was writing this chapter and musing over the space, I was already plotting a bedroom refresh. Life's too short to live with something you don't love.

(above) A console table with vintage vase and Pooky lamp by Matthew in the bedroom of his previous Mallorca home.

(right) The Indian truck sign above the bed in Matthew's former bedroom in Mallorca was picked up on one of his many visits to the country. Displayed alongside Indian miniatures, bright lampshades, a kantha bedspread and curtains made from a turquoise throw, it adds to an overall effect evoking the colour-saturated street life of his favourite place to visit.

(opposite and above) Matthew painted the walls of his bedroom in his old house in Deià a 'dirty lilac' colour, an unexpected choice for someone ambivalent about purple. 'In the Balearics you're drawn to doing things a certain way,' he says. 'I wanted to do something that wasn't of its place.'

(above) The Japanese painting seen here was a present to Matthew from his partner Joseph, which he had framed in bright orange to pick out its colours.

(opposite) A red silk upholstered chair for Duresta adds drama and creates a focal point in the space.

(opposite) An appliqué velvet fabric acts as a room divider, with banquette cushions in the same fabric.

(above) A screen for Roome London features outsized ferns and palms in tropical shades that stand out against petrol-blue walls.

(above and opposite) Matthew's 'Sunbird' wallpaper creates a suitably 'over-the-top, gilded feel' in the bridal suite at Aynhoe Park, a 17th-century estate in the English countryside.

'Purple for me feels heavy and dark with an almost sombre quality. It's important to know what you love but equally useful to know what you don't.'

(opposite) Matthew's silk ikat cabinet for Roome London takes pride of place against a rich aubergine wall. 'I don't know if I'd want to live with it, personally,' he says. 'But it makes a very compelling backdrop.'

(above) Don't be afraid of furniture with a sense of humour, such as Matthew's flamingo-leg side table with a neon top, which makes a good talking point.

(opposite) Matthew's 'Oh So Sisco' rug is woven in India using traditional techniques. The purple and pink tones add depth to the design.

174

Q: Beyond colour, lighting and artworks, do you have any DIY insider tips on how to elevate a space?

A: These are a few easy-to-achieve tricks I've picked up along the way from stylish homes, hotels and restaurants I've visited and have now adopted at home for myself.

A new perspective. Take a moment in a space you are very familiar with and try to see it with fresh eyes and a new perspective. Easier said than done I know, as we all get stuck in a rut sometimes and favour the familiar, but just for a second imagine what your room might look like if you flipped everything around for a different feel. Moving furniture costs nothing and can sometimes be just the trick for an instant refresh. Ask a friend to help as they can often see things differently and might bring some fresh ideas to a space they see less frequently.

Bedtime bliss. Add a small bud vase or even just a jam jar with a few sprigs from the garden to a bedside table. Stack four pillows upright against the headboard and fold back the top of the duvet and add a blanket to the bottom third of the bed. This always looks smart and adds a luxurious touch. Clear any clutter, add a water carafe on a side table and bedroom slippers on a mat. You'll soon feel like you're staying at a fancy hotel and sleep like a well-looked-after guest.

(opposite) A bedroom with two-toned bedspread designed by Matthew and inspired by pressed flowers.

Go green. Flowers and plants are always a good way to enhance the feel of a space. Like living sculptures, plants can act like art and make a statement. Think about large branches of foliage. They're more hardy, so last longer than flowers, and can make a dramatic impact. Pick an evergreen branch from the garden at least six times larger than you would perhaps initially think. Sit it in a terracotta pot and enjoy its oversized sculptural form for weeks if not months to come. Plants and flowers will of course add life to a space and a plant in every room is always a good idea. Counting them up in my own home as I write, there's a large potted faux tree in my lounge by a bay window, an architectural succulent sat in my bathroom and cooking herbs potted in terracotta pots on a kitchen window sill.

Coffee table tricks. The truth is, I usually like my coffee table pretty clear as it's there primarily for the family to congregate around when a dinner table setting feels too formal. To avoid the inevitable daily pile of items stacking up we have a console table with drawers at the front door and an oversized bowl that at once hides keys, sunglasses and wallets from sight, and is also where things that get lost are usually found. If guests come to visit that's another story, as I like to dress the coffee table so it's a welcoming focal point in the room. Creating two or three platforms of hardback books is a classic way to elevate and highlight items. A decorative box is always handy for hiding remote controls, and a tray for setting out nuts or olives. A large piece of coral and a glass paperweight add texture and intrigue. Set a candle atop the book pile too and the transformation is complete.

Drinks station. Much like a morning breakfast bar, an evening drinks station is an easy and affordable way to add some glamour and a decadent touch to your space. Whether you drink or not, it's a lovely touch to add to a lounge space for an air of sophistication and to have drinks close to hand for any impromptu visitors. In my home I've used a 1970s Italian brass bar cart to set the scene. The lower shelf is reserved for a box of chocolates, breadsticks and crackers alongside small plates and a serving tray, while the glass top is loaded with bottles.

Treasure vignettes. This is an inexpensive and weekly routine in my home. I'm always moving things around, part styling, part rearranging. I believe every room needs a little attention once in a while (if not every week) to shake things up. There are no rules to follow other than to gather what you love. You'll need a flat surface, which could be a chest, a shelf or a hard chair seat. Arrange what you want to highlight on the surface, stand back and view it from a couple of angles in the room. A grouping of three objects usually works well. I'd include a portable table lamp, some foliage and a third object that you particularly want to highlight. I usually do these vignettes in so-called dead spaces, such as under the stairs.

'From classic and conservative to bold and electric, not to mention powdery and pale, there's definitely the perfect shade of blue to suit every taste.'

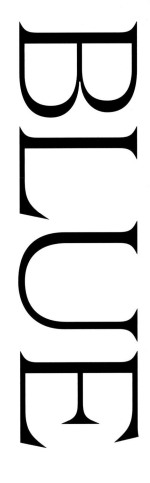

A way from the perils of purple, I'm back in my happy place when it comes to blue. Who can possibly not feel happy thoughts when thinking of the colour blue? I wonder. With so many positive connotations and associations, it takes me instantly in my mind's eye to crisp blue skies and glistening deep blue sea. In a similar way to green, blue is a colour I associate mostly with nature, and specifically summer. It's got that feel-good factor and its possibilities are endless. It's an expansive colour we see in nature each and every day so as a familiar tone to our eye it's no wonder we are naturally drawn to it. It's easy and polite, without being boring, and a harmonious colour to live with.

The scope for using blue in the home is huge. From French blue to cornflower you can tread very gently and dip your toe in the water, through to azure and aqua for actual watery shades with a more vibrant thread. I love all these tones but none more so than the deepest indigo blues and sapphires through to Klein Blue and electric blue for a brilliantly bold statement. When creating a blue-based colour palette for an interior refresh, you might not need to look very far for inspiration. Take a blue – any blue for

(above) Matthew relaxing in the courtyard of Ibiza interior design store Sluiz.

(right) Matthew's peacock-feather cushion for John Lewis is an extension of his wallpaper for Osborne & Little, seen in the background.

that matter – and the chances are you might just have the perfect shades right under your nose.

There's a timelessness to blue too. Unlike some other colours, blue will never tire or date. It's just not one to fall in and out of fashion. Rather, it's perennially there, whether we're talking clothes or interiors. When not wearing bolder colours myself I tend to wear blue, and it's often navy as it feels classic and failsafe and can be kinder and chicer than black.

I wear it, paint with it, design with it and decorate with it. It's fair to say it's my most commonly used colour. I've painted many wallpaper designs centred around a palette of blue, from a watery pond with lotus flowers to a graphic rendering of peacock feathers in deep blue. Peacocks have been a recurring theme in my work over the years and usually get a touch of electric blue to echo their iridescent chest plumage. It's no surprise that a wallpaper design inspired by a floral meadow featuring a seemingly unending blue sky punctuated with billowing clouds has become my most popular wall covering to date.

Lapis lazuli is probably the most famous natural source of blue, prized for its rich ultramarine colour and historically used by painters for the Virgin Mary's robes. Sourced from Afghanistan and carried along the Silk Road to Europe, it was a hugely expensive material. When it comes to synthetic versions of blue, Prussian blue is the best-recognized name. One of the earliest lab-made pigments, it was invented in Berlin in 1706 by Johann Jacob Diesbach and soon became popular around the world, from France to Japan. Hokusai's famous *Great Wave*, which I adore, is printed in Prussian blue.

Living in Mallorca you can't help but feel the island's preference for blue. Bringing the outdoors in quite literally, there are few homes I've seen that have escaped an interior treatment of one kind of blue or another. Blue threads woven into crisp white linen form the basis of the traditional Mallorcan ikat cloth, which is a popular textile found in many home interiors throughout the Balearic region.

When I first moved to Spain over six years ago, I was commissioned to design a cocktail bar in my village of Deià. The owners had only

one specific request: that the bar be painted in a shade of blue. The rest was up to me. As long as the bar was blue, anything goes! I ramped up their request and decided to go bold. I wanted impact and intensity and a jewel-box feeling and so washed the walls, ceiling and banquette seating in the deepest inky blue. The result was impactful for sure, as guests noted its difference from other familiar shades more often used and seemed to enjoy the decadent feeling of being cocooned in deep, dark blue (pages 184–185).

Back in England I'm using a similar shade of inky blue in another cocktail bar to capture that same atmosphere. All the walls will be clad in my 'Celestia' wallpaper, which features a dark-blue sky with intricately drawn stars etched in gold, falling from the ceiling (pages 190 and 191). Antique brass fixtures will continue the golden theme, as blue and gold can be a winning combination, reminiscent of Old Master paintings and Renaissance interiors. So even though the bolder tones of blue may not necessarily be your taste, rest assured that whatever shade you choose, if you pick the one that speaks most clearly to you it won't let you down.

The first ever dress I made for my debut collection back in 1997 was inspired by those seemingly carefree and clashing tones seen regularly in India. The turquoise draped silk dress, contrasted with cerise pink, was picked from a rack of eleven dresses by Kate Moss, who asked to wear it in my show – and the rest, as they say, is history. My partner noted when I was finishing up writing this book that I should mention this specific shade as he's seen it pop up regularly in my work and in my homes from then right up to the present day. True to form, I'm off now to transform my all-white bathroom inherited from the previous owners with a wash of this very same blue. A vintage turquoise ceramic swan picked up from a local market was all the inspiration I needed for a colour that I know will make the space come to life and spark some joy.

(left) Kate Moss in a look from Matthew's debut 'Electric Angels' fashion show.

(right) This cocktail bar in Deià was put together on a very restricted budget. Electric-blue paint makes for striking walls, with the colour carried over onto the frame of the banquette seating. Most of the furnishings were flea-market finds, and the array of cushions adds interest to the scene.

184

(opposite) The floral wallpaper and the ruched blind
channels 1980s decorating styles in this bathroom that
Matthew completed for a client. 'It's my granniest print,'
he says of the design, which is based on a watercolour.

(above) Matthew's 'Fanfare' wallpaper features Japanese
fans adorned with blossom, koi carp and peacocks.

(above and opposite) The peacock-print bathroom in the
bridal suite at country estate Aynhoe Park in Oxfordshire,
England. Matthew wanted a cocooning effect, so he chose
a single tone from the wallpaper for all the furniture to
unify the space.

(opposite and above) The Star Bar inside the bar in Birmingham, UK, that Matthew recently designed is a smaller, more intimate space. Glass star pendants and star tiles cladding the front of the bar are set against Matthew's 'Celestia' wallpaper for Osborne & Little. The reflective marble countertop shimmers in the gentle light.

(opposite) Matthew's 'Butterfly Wheel' fabric for Duresta
on the sofa chimes with the colours in the painting on
the stairway and the Murano glass chandelier.

(above) The local beach, Cala Deià, was the inspiration
for this cabinet. The design printed onto the cabinet doors
is based on an original painting by Matthew.

(above) Although Matthew has since repainted the walls of his London bedroom a rich green (pages 118–119), the wallpapered chimney breast remains. 'This was me in my most neutral phase,' he says.

(opposite) The sitting room in a residential project that Matthew designed for a client in Cheshire, UK. The client bought the rug as a centrepiece, so Matthew worked from the ground up to design the room around it.

(opposite) Matthew's 'Talavera' wallpaper is a celebration
of the Mediterranean, with oranges, flowers and butterflies
against a sky-blue ground.

(above) The 'Azari' wallpaper was one of the first designs
that Matthew made for Osborne & Little.

'When I think of blue I think of clear blue skies and deep blue seas – associated with nature and summer, it has the feel-good factor.'

(opposite) Matthew's 'Deya Meadow' wallpaper is an imposing choice for a dramatic entrance hall.

(above) A view from the kitchen towards the bathroom
in Matthew's previous home in Deià. The blue door on
the left hides the washing machine and the tiny lobby
is papered in the 'Talavera' wallpaper.

(opposite) The terrace of the suite Matthew designed
at La Residencia hotel in Mallorca. His 'Azari' fabric
has been used as a tablecloth.

(left) The lounge in Matthew's former home in Deià. This room was his attempt at Balearic white and blue living. 'I'm not used to white – it feels quite alien to me – but it was something I really wanted to try,' he says. 'It's not your typical clinical white, after all.' The soft-mint beams tie the room and its furniture together.

Q: What would you say are the main common pitfalls and things to avoid with interior design?

A: Not having a plan before you begin any renovation or home improvement is the most common oversight in my experience and is often why I'm called in to help. Starting with your design DNA board as set out in the Find Your Style chapter will set you on the right path.

Overspending is also all too easy to do. Set a realistic budget and make sure that what you intend to spend is realistic for the work you hope to achieve. Work within your means and try not to cram in too much on a budget that won't stretch, as you could be left with unfinished work, which is never rewarding. Keep a tight rein on your spending and always add in a contingency budget, as it's usually required, in my experience.

Don't be afraid to ask for help – if not with physical work then at least for the occasional chat to bounce ideas back and forth. Choose someone whose taste you admire, who likes design and who will support your ideas and help with any indecision. Even if you disagree it's good to voice your opinion and hear opposing ones, as this can sometimes help to crystallize ideas and to take on board those of someone you trust.

Looking too far afield and straying from your design vision is also quite common and I often fall foul of this myself. With social media pulling you this way and that it's tough to stay on track. Remember, your home is primarily for you and should address your needs and tastes. Take inspiration from others, as that's a natural part of the process, but enjoy developing your own unique style. You're the one who has to live there, after all!

(above) Matthew at work painting the wallpaper in the lounge of his previous home in Mallorca.

2 *and* **4** Matthew Williamson · **6** Paul Raeside/Living Etc/Future Publishing Ltd · **8** Lynne Harkes **11–12** David Williamson · **13** The Manchester School of Art Slide Library at Manchester Metropolitan University Special Collections Museum · **14** Jonathan Glynn-Smith · **15** *(top)* Ray Okudzeto **15** *(bottom)* Eric Meola/Getty Images · **16** *(top)* Stefan Rousseau/PA Archive · **16** *(bottom)* Kayt Jones/ Art + Commerce · **17** Matthew Williamson · **22–23**: *1.* Matthew Taylor/Alamy Stock Photo; *2.* Ed Buziak/Alamy Stock Photo; *3.* Fredrika Lökholm; *5.* Henri Matisse, *Harmony in Red*, 1908, The State Hermitage Museum. © Succession H. Matisse/DACS 2023; *6.* dpa picture alliance/Alamy Stock Photo; *7.* Vinyls/Alamy Stock Photo; *9.* Brent Hofacker/Alamy Stock Photo; *10.* Orbon Alija/ Getty Images; *11.* Y H Lim/Alamy Stock Photo; *12.* Amanpuri, Thailand; *13.* Soho House & Co; *14.* David Sandison/The Independent/Alamy Stock Photo; *16.* Tim Graham/Getty Images; *19.* Matthew Williamson (watch), Skye Velosa (drawing) · **26** *(top)* Matthew Williamson · **26** *(bottom)* Peter Cassidy · **27** *(top)* Peter Cassidy · **27** *(bottom)* Horst P. Horst, Vogue © Condé Nast · **28** Simon Upton/ The World of Interiors/Condé Nast · **29** Peter Cassidy · **30–31** Karolina Kuc · **32–33** Paul Raeside/ Living Etc/Future Publishing Ltd · **34** Matthew Williamson · **35** Damian Russell · **36** Matthew Williamson · **37** Damian Russell, artwork by Georg Kitty · **38** Germán Saiz/Original photography for AD, Architectural Digest Spain · **39** Iaia Cocoi · **40** Paul Raeside/Living Etc/Future Publishing Ltd · **41** Damian Russell · **42** Enkel Art Studio · **44** Damian Russell · **45** Turner Bianca · **47** Cassie Nicholas · **50** *(top)* Dan Lecca · **50** *(bottom)* Renard Press · **51** *(top)* Peter Cassidy · **51** *(bottom)* Obeetee · **52** Iaia Cocoi · **53** Matthew Williamson · **54–56** Karolina Kuc · **57** Simon Upton/ The World of Interiors/Condé Nast · **58–59** Tom Mannion · **60–62** Iaia Cocoi · **62** artwork by Alan Hydes · **64–65** Iaia Cocoi · **66** Matthew Williamson · **67** Osborne & Little · **68–69** Iaia Cocoi **70–71** Matthew Williamson · **72** Duresta · **73–75** Iaia Cocoi · **77** Cassie Nicholas · **80** *(top)* Sotheby's · **80** *(bottom)* Arthur Elgort/British Vogue/Condé Nast · **81** David Miller/Abaca Press/ Alamy Stock Photo · **82–83** Karolina Kuc · **84–87** Damian Russell · **88** Tom Mannion · **89** Lynne Harkes · **90–91** Tom Mannion · **92** and **94** Damian Russell · **95** Obeetee · **96–97** Iaia Cocoi **98–99** Damian Russell · **100–101** Duresta · **103** Matthew Williamson · **106** *(top)* Iaia Cocoi **106** *(bottom)* Helena Gurowitsch · **107** Damian Russell · **108** Cassie Nicholas · **109** Tom Mannion · **110–111** Karolina Kuc · **112** Lynne Harkes · **113** Tom Mannion · **114** Tim Beddow/ The World of Interiors/Condé Nast · **115** Iaia Cocoi · **117** Tim Beddow/The World of Interiors/ Condé Nast · **118–119** Damian Russell · **120** Rachael Smith/The World of Interiors/Condé Nast · **121–126** Damian Russell · **127** Osborne & Little · **128** Damian Russell · **129** Obeetee **130–131** Damian Russell · **133** Lynne Harkes · **136** *(top)* Delaware Art Museum (Samuel and Mary R. Bancroft Memorial, 1935) · **136** *(bottom)* Dan Lecca · **137** Damian Russell · **138–139** Karolina Kuc · **140** Damian Russell, artwork by Florence Hutchings · **141** Damian Russell, artwork by Jonathan Schofield · **143** Obeetee · **144** Osborne & Little · **145** Damian Russell · **146** Helena Gurowitsch, artwork by Kate Bellm · **147** Damian Russell · **148** Osborne & Little · **149** Peter Cassidy · **150** Enkel Art Studio · **151** Osborne & Little · **152** Helena Gurowitsch · **153** Osborne & Little · **155** Helena Gurowitsch · **158** *(top)* GRANGER-Historical Picture Archive/Alamy Stock Photo · **158** *(bottom)* Damian Russell · **159–161** Karolina Kuc · **162–166** Iaia Cocoi **167** Duresta · **168** Osborne & Little · **169** Roome London · **170–171** Holly Falconer · **173** Roome London · **174** Duresta · **175** Obeetee · **177** Lewis Rhodes, art direction Adam Nowell, styling Hannah Bort · **180** *(top)* Joseph Velosa · **180** *(bottom)* Damian Russell · **181** © Robert Fairer **182–183** Karolina Kuc · **184–185** Matthew Williamson · **186–187** Osborne & Little · **188–189** Holly Falconer · **190–191** Damian Russell · **192** Duresta · **193** Roome London · **194** Matthew Williamson **195** Cassie Nicholas · **196–197** and **199** Osborne & Little · **200** Matthew Williamson · **201** Tom Mannion · **202–203** Iaia Cocoi · **205** Joseph Velosa

The author wishes to thank the following:

Jos van Raak, Lia Briannte, Kate Bellm, Molly Coath, Katharina at Heroldian Art, Lynne Harkes, Michelle Oguhendin, Sienna Miller, Daniele Roa, Enkel Art Studio, Damian Russell, Iaia Cocoi, Karolina Kuc, Amanda Pickett, The Pickleson Paint Co., Roome London, Sonja Burri, Cara Ward, Laura Morris, Victoria Sanders, Joseph Velosa and Skye.

Special thanks to my editor Augusta Pownall for commissioning, hand holding and having faith in this book.

FRONT COVER: Damian Russell
BACK COVER: *(top left)* Damian Russell; *(top right)* Osborne & Little; *(portrait)* James D. Kelly

Chapter opener prints throughout are by Matthew Williamson

First published in the United States of America in 2023 by Chronicle Books LLC.

First published in the United Kingdom in 2023 by Thames & Hudson Ltd, 181A High Holborn, London WC1V 7QX

ISBN 978-1-7972-2774-0

Printed and bound in China by C&C Offset Printing Co. Ltd

Chronicle Chroma
An Imprint of Chronicle Books

www.chroniclechroma.com